AUG   2007

364.1536 DE MILLY
DE MILLY, WALTER.
IN MY FATHER'S ARMS :A
 TRUE STORY OF INCEST /
2007/06/07

D0016187

WITHDRAWN

In My Father's Arms

LIVING OUT
Gay and Lesbian Autobiographies

Joan Larkin and David Bergman
GENERAL EDITORS

In My Father's Arms

A TRUE STORY OF INCEST

Walter de Milly III

Alameda Free Library
1550 Oak Street
Alameda, CA 94501

The University of Wisconsin Press

The University of Wisconsin Press
2537 Daniels Street
Madison, Wisconsin 53718

3 Henrietta Street
London WC2E 8LU, England

Copyright © 1999
The Board of Regents of the University of Wisconsin System
All rights reserved

3   5   4   2

Printed in the United States of America

Library of Congress Cataloging-in-Publication Data
De Milly, Walter.
In my father's arms: a true story of incest / Walter de Milly III.
144 pp.   cm.—(Living out)
ISBN 0-299-16510-8 (cloth: alk. paper)
1. De Milly, Walter.   2. Incest victims—Florida—Tallahassee
Biography.   3. Male sexual abuse victims—Florida—Tallahassee
Biography.   4. Adult child sexual abuse victims—Florida—
Tallahassee Biography.   5. Incest—Florida—Tallahassee
Case studies.   6. Fathers and sons—Florida—Tallahassee
Case studies.   I. Title.   II. Series.
HV6570.8 T35 D45   1999
364.15'36—dc21
[B]   99-6275

I dedicate this book to my mother and sister,
whom I thank for allowing me to tell my story.
Your courage and love sustain me.

Things are not always what they seem.
—*Phaedrus*

Acknowledgments

I AM GRATEFUL TO MY FRIENDS WHO ENCOURAGED, PUSHED, UNDER-stood, taught, nudged, waited, criticized, nourished, and put up with me until the book was finished. Thank you.

For editorial help I thank Wallace Floyd, Frank Taylor, Richard Browner, David Groff, and Louise Quayle.

To Tim Roeder and Chuck Pearson, thank you for being my friends and supporting me in every way throughout these years.

To Captain Tom, thank you for taking me out to the green waters those days when I've needed it most.

To Lewis and Manny, my "older brothers," thank you for making me part of your lives.

To Larry, Jorge, the late Mark B., Mark S., Kevin K., thank you more than I can say. To all my Tallahassee friends, especially Ashby Stiff, Peter Munton, and Tom Hicks, thank you.

To the psychiatrists and researchers who took the time to help me, especially Dr. Linda Cooper Miles, who first "discovered" the source of my father's pedophilia, thank you.

To my Key West extended family, I love you all: Greg B., John, Richard, Travis, Ted, Blue, Dean, Paul, Michael M., David, Mark, and Danny, Jimmy M., Bill N., Eric N., and Louis.

To Alex of the Black Forest, thank you for your magic.

To Shawn and David, thank you for your love.

Michael Dively, thank you for your consistent support and your challenges, especially at the end, when it was so hard for me to let go.

For helping me survive the most extraordinary darkness, I thank Steve Torrence and Dr. William Hawthorne.

For treating me with kindness and respect, and for inspiring me, I thank the Key West literati, especially Joy Williams, Ross Claiborne, Bill Wright, and the late John Malcolm Brinnin.

And to the teachers, friends, and helpers from my past, I remember you always: Ruth Skretting, Dr. Linville, Dr. Oliver, John Rising Watson, Carol Ouzts, J. Michael Carrin, Ed Cake, Sally, Tom, Payne, Bud, and Jim.

This story has been nearly impossible to tell. On one hand, the purpose of this book is to tell the truth. Yet doing so *exactly* would embarrass or hurt many innocent people. So I have omitted certain individuals altogether, substituted fictitious or composite characters for real ones, and obfuscated their roles in ways that hide their identities. This story has been impossible to tell for another reason: my memory is imperfect. There are still voids of time in my past. When I was writing this book, even I wondered at times whether any of it was true. But it was true, and the hard facts are confirmed in letters, reports, and taped conversations.

Part One

1

THE MORNING AFTER PRESIDENT KENNEDY TOLD THE NATION ABOUT Cuba's nuclear missile sites, my father went to his office at the bank and began hunting for plans to build a bomb shelter.

Five months later, one of the largest private bunkers in Tallahassee sat at the back of our house. It awed me. I gawked at the five deadbolts on the heavy lead door. I could hardly comprehend the yard-thick concrete walls. But what fascinated me most was the only window: a port the size of a shoe box so thick with glass blocks that it dimmed even the brightest sun. If I stood on my toes, I was just tall enough to peer into the swimmy, ice-green glow. No matter how I turned and tried to see, the world outside made no sense.

I imagined life in the midst of war. X-rays broke like brittle arrows against the fortress walls. Inside, Mother cooked on a camp stove. Dad cranked the air pump. Grandmother read a fairy tale about a wolf and a fox to my sister and me, and then we listened, all of us together, while a radio announcer reported on the war and finished by saying, "All we can do is pray."

I could feel the softened shock of bombs exploding in the back yard. With three feet of sand overhead, I thought, nothing can destroy this place. Not even Russian soldiers can break in.

But Dad and I had privileges. Nearly every morning he stopped by my bedroom, woke me, and took me to the bunker. This was father and son time at the de Milly house.

He stripped off his pajamas and hung them on the knob to a cabinet door. Then, standing nude on the bare floor, he faced me and began his calisthenics. As always, I sat on a bunk, watching. He fascinated me, in the way any nine-year-old might be enamored and impressed by his father.

"How come you always do jumping jacks?" I asked.

"Because a man needs exercise."

"I mean, why do you always do jumping jacks?"

"Watch me. Did I tell you I used to do one-arm pull-ups?" Dad flexed his biceps. "See?"

"Yeah. You've told me that a thousand times." I looked at his arm. Dad had a tan, even in winter, but when he flexed his biceps the skin stretched pale and thin.

"How come we have a window if you can't see out of it?"

"So we can tell if it's night or day."

"Why would it matter? There's nothing we could do about it if we were locked in here all the time."

"Well, you'd know when it was time to sleep. And maybe it helps to know that the world goes on."

"I guess." This early in the morning, before the sun, the window-port sat dark and deep.

One morning after Dad finishes his workout, he pulls a fold-down bunk from the wall and lies down, still unclothed. I sit on the floor beside him. I watch his erection. He slaps his tummy with it. He laughs as if he is surprised. "Touch it," he says, holding his penis up, offering it to me. I reach over, hold it with my fingers, and let it go, making a thwack.

He laughs. "Now I'll look at yours," he says. "Stand up." He pulls my pajamas down. He holds my penis between his thumb and forefinger and squeezes.

"Don't," I say.

"I want to make sure it's growing right," he tells me. He studies it, he hums, he tugs and twists.

"Let go." I try to force his hand away.

He ignores me, but then he eases back on his strokes and lies down on the bunk. He pulls at his own penis. He closes his eyes. I watch him, see his lips tighten into thin lines. He lies flat, grim, as if he is extracting some splinter from deep within himself.

I stand by the bunk. I have seen his penis before when it is hard. He'd tried to put it into my bottom. He is going to do it again, isn't he?

"I don't want to be here," I say. "Unlock the door. Please, Daddy."

The bunker sits around me, heavy and grotesque.

I disappear.

Another Walt opens his blue eyes, reverent, paralyzed, the minutes stroking past, father rocking, breathing, bearing upon things the boy cannot understand. Arteries throb at his father's temples. White liquid shoots from the man's penis. The boy backs away, afraid, hurting, choked. The shelter closes in on him. He runs to the door and jumps up to reach the highest bolt, the only one his father locked. He jams his finger turning it.

He runs through the house fast, darting by the kitchen, afraid to look at his mother, afraid that she'll see the naughtiness in his face. And he is certain that his daddy will come running after him with a belt.

The boy runs into his room, falls face down on his bed, and wishes he would die. He waits to die, his nose pressed against the sheet, his eyes cold and still. He waits without moving until he hears his father leave the house. Then the boy rises from the bed. He drifts toward the bedroom window. The glass shines hard. Outside, the morning sun hides behind a sassafras tree.

He watches his father walk along the driveway, carrying his blazer over his arm, tie tight and kempt, his white shirt crisp against his Presbyterian back. The boy watches as the man gets in the car and backs it out to the street. The boy digs his fingernail into the window sash and peels away the varnish. He lets out a breath. He stands all alone and he wants to stay alone. He doesn't want his father to ever come back.

His mother comes to the bedroom.

"Son," she says, surprised to see him still in pajamas, "you're going to be late. Get dressed and let's go!"

Walt inspects his fingernail.

"Did you hear me?" she asks with a rising voice.

He doesn't answer.

"Yes," I mumble, waking up.

I put on my school clothes. I examine my finger, as if it has been injured. I wonder why it hurts, not quite able to think clearly but curious nevertheless and certain that something is wrong with it.

I say nothing when Mother and Caroline and I climb into the car and start off to school. In those days we don't have seat belts, but Mother makes us lock the doors. The drive takes a few minutes.

By the time I sit down in my classroom, I am gone to somewhere new. My teacher soon notices my wayward gaze. "Pay attention, Walt." But her call is not enough to make me let go of what I have. My eyes are fixed on the windows, the perished morning, the far light of God.

2

OUR BEACH CABIN SITS ATOP A SUGARY-WHITE SAND DUNE AT THE SOUTH-
ern boundary of raw, simple country, the pine woods and great savannas
of northern Florida. A state road a half-mile inland follows the coastline.
Cars pass infrequently, their whine burning through the sky.

From its walls the cabin gives a faint, even historic, scent of marsh
grass and rusty bed springs. Army bunks sit everywhere, even on the
front porch. The hallway descends into photographs of my father, my
grandfather, my nine-fingered great-grandfather, their wives and their
boats and their children. Faded inscriptions say, "Papa with his boat,
1913," "Summer, 1955: Pat frying the big trout that daddy caught," "The
children, July 4th, 1960. (Little David is in bed sick)."

It is my seventh year, the summer of 1960. Mother takes my sister
Caroline and me on a long walk, down to the marshes' edge. In the
afternoon wind the saw grass bows to the land. Sandbars swell and ripple.
A carpet of fiddler crabs appears, stopping to flutter in place. They hum
and they crackle.

"Honey," Mother says to me, "behind your ankle. There!"

I turn around and pick up a crab with an iridescent lavender shell and
long-stalked, wiggling eyeballs. I hold it to Mother's face.

"My goodness!" she exclaims. "That's a pretty one. You wonder who
he's looking at!" She smiles a silly smile, slants her head with the crab's,
and rolls her eyes.

The crab sits on my palm. I look at its claws. One is tiny and the other
is enormous, bigger than its shell.

"God sure does make peculiar creatures," Mother says as she cups her
hand under mine.

I think of God as an old man putting pieces of crab together. "Do you
think God made it this way on purpose?" I ask.

"Why I'm sure he did," she says. "Don't you think it's pretty?"

"Yeah," I say, holding the single large claw. But I think God made a mistake. Maybe he really tried, but his fingers were just too big and he gave up halfway through.

My sister has found another crab and hurries it into a plastic bucket. "Mama," she yells, "look!"

Mother takes my sister's hand in hers while they both bend over to watch the tiny crab trot sideways around the edge.

"Can I take mine to Cub Scouts?" I ask her.

"No, Mommy," says Caroline, "he'll let it go in the house and it'll die somewhere and start stinking, like those hermit crabs he caught last year."

"Well . . ." Mother says to me. "If I let you take him, you'll have to bring him right back here and let him go."

For a moment she stands nobly, filled with power and beauty. I am amazed. We turn back toward the cabin. Caroline swings the bucket in her hand and looks into it again and again.

"Let's name him," she says. "Let's name him Purple." We decide we're going to set up a little house for Purple. We run ahead of Mother, up the path to the cabin, flying to the front porch. We fling open the screen door and find Dad painting the window sill; we show him the crab.

"I got it," I announce.

"No, you didn't," Caroline says. "I got it."

"Well, go get some salt water and sand so he can have a place to burrow into," Dad tells us.

"How come?" I ask.

"He needs a place to sleep," Dad says. "He sleeps in his burrow."

Together we swoop down to the shore and hurry back to make Purple's home. We put the bucket atop the old tube radio. Mother sets up a card table and gives Caroline and me a mountain lake jigsaw puzzle.

We can put it together while she makes sandwiches. This is our quiet hour. I wait at the table, searching for the edges, purring. I love her so much.

My mother grew up in polite Southern society, protected by her parents from the vulgar and the base. But she fully understood human beings' capacity to cause horror. In a speech against war in her college years, she addressed the audience like a mother who is waking a child from a dream. Exquisitely sensitive to the necessity of patriotism, effusing sweet idealism, her speech about World War II got the attention of the local paper. It printed the text, gushing as hometown papers are apt to.

Her consciousness was formed in the embrace of a bright, accomplished, religious family. They had come to Florida from the Tennessee country, at the northeastern border, a place some call the Lost State of Franklin. Nearly every generation of her ancestors occupied high office—senators, governors, and a commissioner of Indian affairs, Nathaniel Taylor. He admonished the army for its stupidity in slaughtering the Indians on every possible occasion. What he wanted most was for the Indians to maintain their culture.

"He fought to keep Native Americans under the jurisdiction of the Department of the Interior," Mother told me. "But Congress had other ideas. Upon his departure from office they put the Indians under control of the War Department. Isn't that awful? They're just like children up there."

She mothered us in the fifties, a time when the word *pedophile* did not exist in the vocabulary of fine Christian women. For that matter, no word or phrase connoting any sex act could, or would, be spoken by my mother or any of her friends.

So she did not know that people like my father existed, certainly not before marriage, not even after my sister and I were born. He concealed from her his worship of me. But clues emerged in my childhood, vague indifferences on my part, lost gazes and long measureless breaths, which, on the afternoon of my twelfth birthday party in December 1965, sent me skulking off from my friends. Mother found me behind the house, crying for reasons I couldn't explain. And I did other things that worried her.

As I would learn thirty years later, she took those clues, and Dad, up the street to a psychiatrist, Dr. Saunders. Practicing at a time when father-son incest was unheard of—and prompted by fears that I would be irrevocably "marked" as a psychiatric patient—he dismissed my idiosyncrasies as a passing sadness, best left for me to deal with alone.

Mother didn't dumbly accept his opinion. She went to the state library to find books on child development and psychology. She read everything she could find. But the literature did not tell about the kinds of fathers who pierce their sons with lies and terror. Psychologists considered incest—and the mental disturbances arising from it—so rare that it would have taken twenty towns the size of Tallahassee to incubate just one guilty father. Even then, such a father would not have fit the description of Walter de Milly.

3

IN A COOL, CRINKLY SEERSUCKER SUIT, MY FIFTY-YEAR-OLD FATHER WALKS along the main street of Tallahassee, headed toward his office at the bank. He comes upon a childhood friend who has never had much luck earning a living. In the moment of recognition, my father nearly leaps into a state of delight. His brows jump above glittering eyes. His jaw drops. He pauses, collecting the other man fully.

"Well, Tom Jay Sanders!" he exclaims in a knowing voice, as if a joke is on the way.

Tom Jay laughs. "Hello, Mister de Milly."

"How have you been getting along?" my father asks.

"Oh, just fine," says Tom Jay. "And you?"

"Fine." At this point, Southern manners would allow my father to say goodbye and resume his walk, but he stays, and Tom Jay waits.

"So, how do your job prospects look?" Dad asks.

"Well, I haven't found anything much lately," Tom Jay responds.

"I bet if you go see Mister Evans over at his construction company," my father tells him, "he might have something for you. He's building fifteen new houses out at Buck Hill Estates."

"Well, thank you, Mister de Milly," Tom Jay says and breaks into a smile.

"You're a fine man, Tom Jay."

Now the man beams. Dad goes on to the bank, and he calls up Evans, to whom he's lent the construction money. "If Tom Jay comes to see you about a job," my father says, "I'd like for you to hire him." Evans obliges.

Although my father has imposed on Evans, as he did with other local businessmen, the community's assessment of my father would rise with each such call. After all, how many bankers would go out of their way to help the disadvantaged?

To my young eyes, my father occupied a station of influence somewhere in the upper air, beyond rank or title, beyond his birthright as a gentleman of the Southern tradition. He hadn't inherited any real wealth, much less accumulated it. He didn't own the bank. And he never occupied public office. But everyone in town knew him, and everyone somehow owed him approval. He was always giving his time to the community: establishing a new Presbyterian church. Raising the money to build a four-hundred-acre Boy Scout camp. Hearing cases as a member of the ethics committee of the Florida Bar. But these were the effects of his power, not the source. What my father seemed to possess was a kind of magnificent intimacy with his community: he knew every house, every parcel of land, every family. Sometimes I thought he knew the history of every tree in the county. It was as if, in some mysterious way, in some timeless summer long ago, he had been to see everyone. He'd offer his fellowship for no apparent reason, though often there was one: counsel, compassion, or money to build a new house.

The community was more than appreciative. People seemed to hold a place in their hearts for him, and they let me know it. Hardly a week went by without someone telling to me, "Your father is the finest man I've ever met." After I was grown, someone made me remember it wasn't true. In the mid-1980s the Ashwoods moved into the neighborhood. Their son, ten-year-old Kenny, soon met my father and became his friend.

Kenny Ashwood glared down at the table, said nothing, pushed his dinner plate away, and marched up to his bedroom. His mother thought that whatever was bothering her son was nothing more than a child's quandary, a problem Daddy could fix. When his father went to ask what was wrong, Kenny said, "It's just what Mister de Milly keeps doing when we play."

"What's that?" his father wanted to know.

Kenny trembled and dropped his head. His hands rested on his thighs. "Mister de Milly always grabs me down here." Kenny's right finger leaned in a hint of movement toward his crotch.

Like other children who knew my father, Kenny loved him. Where other men often treated children with a kindly sort of indifference, Walter de Milly gave children his direct, enthusiastic attention. He teased them, he made silly faces, and he took them seriously when they talked.

Kenny had often come by our house after school. Lately, Dad had been teaching the boy how to tie nautical knots. Kenny had already mastered the square knot, memorizing the formula: "Right over left and under, left over right and under."

Now Kenny told his father what had happened earlier that day. Mr. de Milly had taken Kenny to the garage. My dad sat on the doorstep and laid a short length of heavy nylon line across his knees.

"Here," he said, holding the end of the line between his fingers and talking through the steps as he formed a knot. "Here's the rabbit. It comes out of the hole, under the limb, and back into the hole." Dad pulled the knot snug. "See?"

Kenny leaned against Dad's knee and tried it himself. He made the hole backward and the knot fell apart.

"Come here," Dad said. He wedged Kenny between his knees and reached around, holding the line so the boy could see.

"Watch how I do this. You make the loop away from you." Dad flipped the rope over itself and tied the knot again. Then Kenny, his unsure fingers taking the line through the turns, made the loop right. "Atta boy!" Dad said. Deft and sure at the age of seventy, he tickled Kenny with one hand, while the other grabbed the boy's groin.

Kenny giggled, then tried to wiggle loose.

"No!" he screamed, squirming. Dad laughed.

"No!" Kenny screamed. Dad laughed, digging his fingers into the boy's side.

"No!" Dad let go. Kenny pushed himself away. He dropped the knot on the floor. "I've got to go home. It's time for dinner."

"You tell your daddy that you can tie a bowline," Dad said, unperturbed, his eyes as wide as a boy's and just as delighted. Kenny walked away; when he got out of Dad's sight, he stomped; on toward his house he crashed past green hedges and bumblebees.

That night in 1985 Mr. Ashwood called me.

"Do you know what your father is? Do you know what he did to my son?" His voice shook.

"No, sir," I said.

"Your father molested my son," he said.

With these strange yet predictable words, I fell into darkness. I stood holding the phone, not feeling it in my hands, thinking, disengaged from the world, cool, strategizing, analyzing. I must calm him, I thought. He's crazy.

"Did you hear me?" he asked.

"Yes," I said, in my most formal voice, "but are you sure? Are you serious?"

"I'm serious as hell. If your father were anyone else, if it weren't for your mother, I'd have the police over here right now. But as long as your father does what I say, no one has to know about this."

"I don't think you have to worry," I said.

He ignored me. "If your father doesn't do what I say, I will call the police, I will press charges."

"What do you want?" I asked. "You want me to talk to him about it? I'll tell him to leave Kenny alone."

"That's not enough," he said. "I want your dad to see a psychiatrist. Immediately. And I want his word that he will stay away from my children. All the children on our street. If he won't do this, Walt, if I catch him even looking at my son, I'll call the police. And I will press criminal charges. I don't care who your father is."

"Yes, sir," I said. "I'm sorry. I'll handle this. Dad will listen to me."

"He better. Look, I don't want to report this. I don't want my son to get branded by publicity. But I want your father to know I'm damn serious."

"Okay," I said. I didn't believe his line about my mother. I knew why he had called me instead of Dad. He didn't want to face my father.

But right now, that didn't matter. I couldn't see very well. I hurt, I didn't hurt. I couldn't think, not consciously or rationally. As I hung up the phone, I felt angry at Kenny. Moments of nothingness passed. Then I cried.

Suddenly, I had an incredible impulse to tell everyone about Dad. After all these years, I could finally prove that I had not been lying.

I'd tried to tell the truth about my father years before. It was 1972, not long after I'd gone to college. While drifting in bed through that world of near sleep, I fell into another place and time; suddenly, violently, I am lying in a sleeping bag. Dad has his hand around me; no, Dad, leave me alone I hate you. Then I died.

I awoke in my dorm astounded, furious, knowing Dad had done this to me on a camping trip with the Boy Scouts about eight years before. He was real and worse than real. You hypocrite, I thought—not so much because he had molested me but because he'd done it and then, years later, had been so thoroughly, intensely agitated about my homosexuality. So far as I was concerned, he was a homosexual too. I certainly didn't know then that Dad was a pedophile, that he had begun molesting me when I was an infant, that my homosexuality was more probably caused by genetics than his abusive hands.

Not long after this memory surfaced, I went home for a school break. Maybe because I was careless, maybe because I wanted to tell my parents I definitely was gay, I left on my dresser a letter I'd written to my friend Wallace. Later, after the semester ended and I was home again, Dad found the letter and told Mother about it.

When she confronted me, I told her that Dad had molested me as a child and that what he had done had made me gay.

Mother's demeanor disintegrated. "Your father would never do that," she cried. "I refuse to believe this! When?" She stood up, walked around, hands to her face, not waiting for an answer. "You must have dreamed this."

She did not wait for me to recant or for Dad to have chest pains. I went back to the same psychologist she and Dad had sent me to see back in the eleventh grade, after Mother had found my diary, with its pages of budding homosexual anguish.

This psychologist, Dr. Harry Blount, an expert, a specialist in the problems of adolescents, had tried to "cure" me of my homosexuality when I was sixteen, or at least flesh out my dormant heterosexual drives. It was standard practice at the time, and of course his efforts failed.

"Your dream was a fantasy," he told me, "a natural wish for a young homosexual. Your dad is handsome and powerful. Your dream is an unconscious desire." Then he moved in his chair and broke into a booming voice: "You go back to your mother and you TELL her you made the whole thing up." He frightened me. I didn't believe him, but I was afraid of more pain and embarrassment. I was worn out. I did not want to ever have to speak about my private life again, not with Mother or Dad or Harry Blount. If I didn't have to talk about it, maybe they'd leave me alone. So I went home and obeyed his orders.

Because Mother had refused to believe my accusations in the first place, I can't honestly say that she ever gave serious thought to the possibility that Dad was a pedophile. I, on the other hand, continued to believe that he had made me gay.

The day after the call from Kenny's father, I phoned Wallace, with whom I'd remained friends since college. I called Bo, my lover in Key West. I went to see Lewis and Manny, my best friends in Tallahassee. I told them about Kenny.

"Dad's molesting boys," I said. "He did it to Kenny, and he did it to me."

What are you going to do? they asked.

I didn't know. I knew only that I had to decide how to handle this. I'd have to find a psychiatrist.

My first effort failed. The doctor, a beautifully placid woman saddened by my story, didn't explain why, only that she would not feel comfortable dealing with my father. She referred me to a Dr. Phillip Hahn.

I saw him a week later. When I explained my circumstances, his face revealed a childlike amusement, not with the subject of child molestation but with the idea that the man caught doing it had been Walter de Milly. The moment of pleasure seemed inappropriate but also familiar, an almost sadistic idiosyncrasy of all the male psychotherapists I'd known.

He turned sober. "You've made the correct decision in coming to see me," he said, as if he'd been thinking about the problem for years. "Your father has committed grave, criminal acts. You will of course need to confront him."

I studied the man's face but gave no answer.

"How are you doing in all of this?" he asked, clearly directing his concern to me.

"I'm fine," I said, uneasily. "It's difficult, of course, but I think I'm pretty strong."

For a half hour we talked about pedophilia, its uncertain causes, and about the harmonious public life of Walter de Milly. Hahn told me I'd need to convince Dad to come see him. He also tried to prepare me for a crisis I hadn't yet thought of: Mother might be so totally revolted and distraught about his secret that she might want to divorce him.

Why that hadn't occurred to me, I don't know—but the thought of my mother's leaving Dad was simply astonishing.

Dad seemed delighted when I called early Saturday morning and asked him to go for a drive. I believe he thought we were going to discuss our family business. I picked him up in my Jeep and began to meander through a suburb of Tallahassee, then headed southwest, out of town, along a county road. I had no destination in mind, but when we approached a dirt road that seemed oddly inviting, I pulled onto it and stopped at the shore of a lake. If this becomes unendurable, I thought, I'll drive in and end it all for both of us. Then I thought: how stupid. Both of us are good swimmers.

We sat silently. Panes of sky flashed off the water. Cypress trees walked like sylphs around the lake, gray, bleak, dreaming. Dad seemed to be preparing mental notes for a nature hike. I thought about the watch that I took to bed when I was a boy. I would hold it to my eye like a monocle, mesmerized by the glowing radium numbers. I'd read in my science book that the soft green light came from feeble nuclear reactions. I wondered what would happen if the atoms got out of control, if my watch would blow up, or my house, or the whole city of Tallahassee.

Do it, I told myself. Get it over with.

"Dad," I said, turning to him, and speaking with less force than I wanted, "a few weeks ago, I got a phone call from Mister Ashwood."

"You did?" he asked swiftly, smiling. "What did he have to say?"

I looked directly ahead toward the far side of the lake. "He's angry at you," I said as firmly as I could.

"Oh. I see," Dad said with a nearly imperceptible drop in tone. "What's he angry about?" He stared at the water.

I took a breath. "He's angry," I said, "because he says that you put your hands down Kenny's pants—and fondled him." I felt ashamed.

Dad tried to look at me. I dropped my eyes and could see his hands resting on his thighs, his thumbs stepping back and forth.

"Was this true?" I asked, fearfully. "Did you really have your hands down his pants?"

"Yes."

I felt myself blush or tense. I looked into Dad's eyes and could see them changing into a child's.

"It made Kenny very upset," I said, "and Mister Ashwood says that if you don't get treatment, he's going to press criminal charges. Even then, he wants to decide for himself if you're going to be safe with children." I thought for a moment. Dad remained silent. "You did things like that to me too."

"Yes, I know," he said, calmly, "but I hoped—I hoped you'd forgotten about it."

"I did forget," I said. "But when I was in college, I began to remember things."

"Oh." I waited for him to continue, but he said nothing.

"So I found a psychiatrist here," I said. "I told him about this, about Kenny. I want you to make an appointment. And don't even think about putting it off." I was shaking.

Dad smiled, stunned. "You've seen a psychiatrist? You've been busy."

"Of course I've been busy," I said, irritated. "This is not an insignificant development."

Dad let out his breath. "Isn't there another way?"

"Such as?"

"I just won't do it any more," he said.

"I don't believe you," I said, "and neither will Mister Ashwood. It's too late. This is all set up. You've got to go through with it."

Dad looked at me like he was sorry, or pleading. I shook my head. "This is it," I said. "You're going to do it whether you like it or not."

He scanned the lake. A gray owl swooped out of a gray cypress tree. We watched it fly through the underlight and into what seemed like a mist.

"Okay?" I asked, flying too. "You'll go?"

Dad exhaled. "Yep," he said, shaking his head.

Get the hell out of here, I thought. I cranked the Jeep and we backed away. Dad's body lightened, his face nearly rapturous. Either he was blissful about his capture or happy that we had spent a Saturday morning together. I couldn't imagine which.

A few weeks later I met Hahn for the second time. As planned, Dad had been by for a session.

The doctor's voice moved forward, as if to meet me. "Walt," he said, "your dad doesn't understand the grave reality of this situation. When he came in to see me, he was very clear. He doesn't want to tell your mother, and he believes that he doesn't need psychiatric help. He says he's capable of correcting the problem himself. Of course, this lack of insight is common in pedophiles."

He leaned back in his chair, watching me. I realized I was supposed to react to Hahn's complaint. But I could think of nothing to say.

"I think you better talk to him again," Hahn said, "and tell him that he must tell your mother about this."

No, I thought, I don't want to talk to him again. Why can't you handle it? But I knew it was up to me.

"I'll talk to him," I said. "He'll do what I tell him to do. I don't know why, but he minds me like a child."

"Good," Hahn said. "You ought to give him a deadline for telling your mother, and then I want to see them both. You sure you can do this, Walt?"

"Yes."

The next morning I went into Dad's office and closed the door. He sat low in his chair, subdued, fluid, and much into his Jimmy Stewart gentlemanliness, but I could see anger in his blue eyes. "You have to tell Mother before the week is out," I said.

"Doctor Hahn's a cold fish," Dad said, moving his hands as if he were dismissing the thought. "I'm not sure if I like him."

"Give him a chance," I said, feeling embarrassment. "A lot of psychiatrists come across that way. It's part of their method."

Dad looked pained. "I don't know if I can bring myself to tell your mother about this."

"It's your choice," I said, "but if you don't tell her, then there's no way you can get treatment. We can't have any more secrets."

"Why does she have to know? She'll kick me out of the house. She'll divorce me."

"Because," I said, "you've kept it a secret from her, and that's lying. We aren't going to lie to each other any more. Besides, it's going to be impossible for her not to know. Would you rather make me do it?"

"No," Dad said. "I'll have to think about it . . . how to tell her."

"Certainly you can think about it," I replied. "But you have to tell her before the week is out. And the two of you have to go together to see Doctor Hahn. Either you tell her by the end of the week, or I will."

Dad looked surprised. "But what do I say?"

"Everything," I said. "What you did to me and what you did to Kenny. And to any other boys we don't know about. Then I want both of you to see Doctor Hahn and do whatever he says."

"Will you be there with me?"

"Nope. You have to do it on your own."

"She has no idea," Dad said, floating the thought to nowhere.

The next Sunday afternoon, about an hour after my parents usually got home from church, my phone rang. It was Dad. In the background I could hear my mother wailing.

When I got to the house, Mother ran to the front door, sobbing. She rushed toward me as if she were drowning. I recoiled, confused by disgust and guilt and terror.

"God help us! God help us!" she cried. "Oh, Walt, my poor son!"

Her face was red and all pain. She searched my eyes. "Of course you've had so many problems," she said through her tears. "How could you bear it, how could you live after he did that to you?"

I didn't know what to do. I looked at Dad, ten feet away in his coat and tie, hands in his pockets. His expression could have been either "See what you made me do?" or "Help us, son."

"You must have been strong to keep this horrible secret to yourself," she said angrily, "and Caroline too." She turned to Dad and glared, then looked at me. "No wonder she's always been so irritable. Oh dear God," she sobbed, "it's just awful, just awful."

Dad came over and tried to hug Mother. She extended a chilly, resolute hand and pushed him away. For an instant I wondered whether she was acting.

"You are going to see the psychiatrist," she told him firmly. She looked to me for reassurance, still crying, her eyes liquid and red.

"That's right," I said. I felt like I was melting. Suddenly, I was close to Mother and very sorry for her.

"And we're going to get this behind us," she said, "with the help of God." She bent over in her chair, sobbing. I put my arm around her and saw how delicate and unprepared she had been. Dad left the room and came back with a box of tissues. He held them out to her, as if they were all he had left in the world.

4

THE PROSPECT OF BEING SEEN AT A PSYCHIATRIST'S OFFICE DISTURBED my father down to his blood. So, in the weeks that followed his initial consultation, he defended his privacy with a simple ploy: each time he entered the doctor's office, he carried a briefcase. After all, he told himself, he was a businessman.

Dad met with Hahn three more times, taking tests, answering questions, yielding evidence of his emotional organization, his intellectual apparatus, his sexual pathology. And then one day I found Dad sitting at his desk in our office. He'd retired from the bank several years earlier and we'd opened a real estate investment company. Now he looked afraid. He seemed bigger than he ought to. He stared somewhere beyond me, a scorching, frightening, inhuman gaze. "Doctor Hahn thinks he's got to treat me," he said.

"Well, we've already assumed that, Dad."

"You know what he wants to do? He told me that there's an injection treatment—I'd have to get shots of antisex hormones. Weekly." As he said this, his tan vanished. I could see the blood in his cheeks.

"Weekly?" I asked.

"Yes, every damn week."

"But it sounds like a pretty easy way out of this," I said. "What kind of hormones?"

"Estrogen," he said, poking at the word. "Well, it's not going to happen. The nurses would know what they're giving me; they'll talk about me. Everyone in town would know."

"The nurses wouldn't care," I said. "They probably give a hundred shots every day."

"There's something else," he said. He looked at the door, making doubly sure it was closed. "Doctor Hahn came up with another idea.

He thinks I should be castrated. That would fix me, wouldn't it?" His eyes had turned into blue flames.

"Oh," I nodded, trying to think, but I couldn't think of anything.

"It would stop me cold," he said.

"Is that what he says?" I asked.

"He says it would do the job. Then it would be over with."

"But is that what you want to do? I mean, is that it?"

"I don't know," he said, "I'll think about it. It could be a relief, you know." He went on in a singsongy voice, "He sure has got a repugnant attitude. I think he's the wrong doctor." His hands were like forepaws, digging into the arms of his chair.

For the first time, I thought that he might be going crazy. Certainly, Hahn wasn't the wrong doctor. He was just handling Dad the way psychiatrists handle pedophiles. But the idea of castrating my father—that was somehow unthinkable and at the same time eerily familiar. It was as if my body held castration as a memory from long ago, some lost day when he had first gone wrong.

I looked at my father. His hushed panic flooded the room. His luck had come to an end. He was trapped hard and shackled in his own forest. Medicine men flashed in the trees, spitting at the fire. "Smoke follows beauty," Dad had told us boys long ago. But long ago was now; he smoldered in his chair, shamed, and meant to be put out.

Hahn soon asked my family to meet with him. Caroline flew down from Virginia. Mother and Dad drove over together (he brought along his briefcase), and I came in my own car. When we convened in Hahn's waiting room, we must have been a portrait of Victorian mourning, my mother, sister, and I stationed separately and upright, our eyes unfocused in the haze, our expressions lost and unbelieving.

My silver-haired father, on the other hand, looked alive, expectant, beatific, as if he were soothing not only himself but the rest of us. His handsome Anglo-Saxon face radiated his intent: he would triumph over this, he would be kind and generous, a loving father, a perfect gentleman. But he wasn't going to give in, not completely. With his health declining, he hadn't many years left to live. He wasn't about to spend his last days caught in the rifle scope of a psychiatrist. So he would call on his proven gift, the single thing in life he did best: he would smile upon us, he would spread peace upon our troubled waters.

The receptionist ushered us to an empty room to wait. Minutes of silence passed. Finally, Mother spoke. "Caroline, next month when you come back to the beach, do you want me to do the grocery shopping ahead

of time, or would you rather do the shopping while I watch the children?"
My sister rolled her eyes. Mother recoiled in the silent language of pain.

Caroline looked at me. I could read her thoughts: Can you believe
we're having to do this? I hate him! I shook my head. I had my own
problems. Across town I had our multimillion-dollar investment business
to run. We expected some complications, which our stockholders weren't
aware of, and I needed to devote my time to correcting the situation before
our troubles got out of hand.

And I yearned to be at home behind closed doors holding my secret
lover, Bo. My business peers did not know about him and neither did my
family. Although I didn't go to great lengths to pretend to the community
that I was heterosexual, neither did I openly discuss my homosexuality.
I would have experienced no real antipathy if I had lived quietly (that
is, "behaved myself") as a single man. But any male member of an old
Tallahassee family who lived openly with his male lover would have
distressed a good part of the community to the point of mortification.

Hahn suddenly materialized in the doorway of the waiting room,
shrouded in thought and an unbuttoned herringbone jacket. Then his
eyes lit up, as if he recognized the very worst things in each of us. "Why
don't you come into my office?"

We walked down a narrow paneled hallway that smelled of coffee
and suede. One by one we entered a cavernous, dim room. The doctor
pulled his chair from behind his desk. We sat in a curve, like a quintet of
musicians thrown together for an unwilling performance.

Hahn picked at his chin. "Have you come to a conclusion?" the doctor
asked, scanning our faces. We sat in awkwardness. I was not sure what
conclusion the doctor meant. We waited. And waited. Finally, shrugging
his shoulders, he continued. "This family does not communicate. I've
talked with young Walt . . ."

Mother interrupted, speaking earnestly. "Walt has been so good
through all of this, he's carried our whole family through, and he's running
the business too. I think he's been marvelous." Though I could hear my
mother distinctly, I couldn't manage to grasp her meaning.

"Yes. Walt's been a trouper," said Hahn, who looked at Mother with
an amused look I'd seen before. Then, with a menacing stare, he turned
to Dad. "Do you understand, Walter, how grave this is?"

"Yes, I understand," Dad said, trying to find a dignified way to relax
in his chair.

"Then you know we're here to discuss your treatment options. You
know we're here to keep you from going to jail." At these words, Hahn
leaned back in his chair and brushed his palms lightly against his thighs.

"Yes, and I've given it a lot of thought," Dad said, drawing on his customary enthusiasm. "I think I can lick this thing." Dad nodded to the doctor, smiling, concerned.

"You can lick it?" Hahn asked incredulously as he looked directly at Dad.

"Yes, I'm sure of it," Dad said, raising his eyebrows to convey both hope and sincerity. "It's not that big an issue. I know I can do it."

An absurd and embarrassed silence enveloped us. I sensed that everyone was waiting for me. I sat upright in a haze. I knew I had to say something, something mature, evenhanded. "I think what Dad's saying is that now that he's been found out, he'll be on guard; he knows that the next time, he'll really get in trouble. Is that what you're thinking, Dad?" I didn't feel anything. I only hoped that everyone would agree.

Dad smiled at me. "That's right, son. You're a smart boy." I looked at my unpolished shoes and tried to keep from smiling. I imagined a young Solomon boldly contemplating the dilemma.

"I don't think that's enough," my sister said sharply. She looked at Hahn. She'd never met him before. "We have to know that he'll never, ever touch—even want to touch—a child again." Her expression stern, she pushed herself against the air.

"You're right," Hahn said, "Walter is glossing over a very serious criminal problem. He's a pedophile."

Hahn's discussing Dad as if he weren't even in the room underlined the utter impossibility of discussing the subject with my father. There was no direct way to draw him into a serious conversation. Like a naughty little boy who simply couldn't absorb the significance of the bad things he had done, Dad maintained his perplexed and concerned mien.

"Now, I've discussed Walter's treatment options with him, and I think he's told you what I think. I've seen Walter enough to doubt that psychotherapy will change him. The other options are estrogen suppression injections, and an orchiectomy. Castration."

Hahn turned to each of us in an almost dramatic and solemn review. It was as if he was expecting one of us to tell him what should be done next. We were silent.

Finally, Hahn looked at me. "Didn't your father tell you that we were meeting today to discuss castration?"

"Dad and I talked about it," I said flatly. "A little." But I had not said a word to my mother or sister about Dad's treatment options. Their lives seemed so far from mine.

My mother, fidgeting with her dress, distressed, found impassioned words and looked at Hahn: "Yes, Walter told me you had discussed it. He thinks it isn't necessary. But we can absolutely not afford to have anyone else find out about Dad. Let's get this over with. As far as psychotherapy goes, people would know; it's a wonder no one has seen him coming and going to this place. In any case, I don't think therapy would work. And I'm not about to let him go off molesting other children. I'm not going to let him ruin us any more than he already has. I'm prepared to make whatever sacrifice is necessary."

Hahn looked at my sister. Mother watched too, with a worried, sentimental expression. "Caroline," Hahn said in his most gentle voice yet, "you and I haven't spoken together before. What do you say about it?"

Not long after Ashwood's call, I'd confessed the truth to Caroline about my incest. She wasn't surprised. Dad, she told me, had mistreated her in his own ways, mostly by exposing himself to her friends and to her. She'd always been angry at him, so angry that she had gone off to college with the intention of never coming home again. She'd married her college sweetheart, and the two had been living in Virginia for the past twelve years. With two children, they were a beautiful family, far removed from the ugliness back in Tallahassee.

"Well, no one's said anything to me about it, but as far as I'm concerned," Caroline said, avoiding any eye contact with Dad, "it's simple. Dad can't be trusted around children. So I say, do the operation. Let's get this over with." Then she turned to Dad with a glare. It was the closest I'd ever seen her come to rage. I wondered if she was going to bring up her past. But she didn't.

Hahn eyed Dad, checking his reaction. Dad seemed a little sad, but he managed to retain his upright posture, and he recovered his glow of self-confidence.

"Walt," Hahn said to me, "where do you stand on this?"

Numbness gripped me. I hugged my chest tight. I didn't know what to say. I floated somewhere behind my own vision. A voice not my own rose from within me. I listened, and I spoke. "I don't think that psychotherapy would work on Dad. I think he'd go along with whatever the therapist says and pretend to cooperate, but I doubt that therapy, or analysis, will change his desires. And it sounds like the injections are too risky. I think he would unconsciously find ways to avoid the treatment, forgetting to go in for the shots, and he'd be constantly embarrassed, and paranoid, fearful that the nurses would gossip."

"You're right, Walt," Mother said with determination. "I think that Walter simply wouldn't manage to keep his appointments, and we'd always have to be after him, reminding him every time, pushing him to

go. I don't want to have to do that. I've had enough trouble with this."
She began to cry.

"I wouldn't forget," said Dad, half-irritated.

"Dad," I said, smiling gently, "you wouldn't forget deliberately. But
sooner or later, you'd forget. And I bet that eventually you'd try to
convince us that you didn't need the injections any more."

"I don't want them anyway," he told me. He was flushed at the
temples.

"But you have to do something," I said, "or you'll go to jail."

"Well, I'm not going to have injections," he said. "Besides, what would
it be, once a month? In a doctor's office where everyone would see me?
No. I'm not going to do that."

My sister rolled her eyes and looked away, disgusted.

"Doctor Mancuso prefers castration," Hahn said, referring to Dad's
internist. "He thinks the estrogen suppression treatments would be risky,
considering Walter's arteriosclerosis." Hahn had been consulting Mancuso about treatment possibilities. The mere mention of Mancuso's name,
and the thought that this esteemed family doctor knew about Dad, was
enough to make all of us shrink further into our humiliation. "Of course,
castration won't eliminate Walter's sexual drive. It's going to reduce it
substantially, though. And, frankly, considering your dad's psyche, we
can't expect abundant relief from his perversion." Hahn brought his hands
together, as if trapping an insect. "It's fused. He's getting older, less capable
of minding himself. Castration won't change him, other than to reduce the
possibilities of grabbing more children. That's what you want, isn't it?"

I looked at my mother. As she told me later, she'd thought I was
handling this crisis quite well. She'd thought that perhaps something good
could come out from all this ugliness. Maybe, she'd thought, this would
be the thing to impel me from my homosexual lifestyle—unless, of course,
it was all due to genetics.

I turned to Dad. I knew he realized that his time had run out. I knew
he was dying inside. I knew nothing mattered any more.

"Dad," I said through my numbness, "you have no choice. If you
don't do this, I'm going to have to tell Mister Ashwood that you aren't
cooperating. But that's not why I want you to do it. It's just . . . time for
it. You've been doing this all your life. You have to give it up. You have
to." I felt myself falling into a cloud of anaesthesia.

Dad looked at me lovingly. His resolve seemed to have collapsed. I
knew he couldn't have been surprised at my words or my authority. He'd
passed that on to me some time ago, when I was in my late twenties. I
remember a perceptible transition in which he'd relinquished his former

dominance. In a sense, he was, and always had been, in love with me. More important, what the family knew now was that I held a unique moral authority, one I'd earned in childhood. Perhaps it was more of a right than an authority, but I was nevertheless entitled to impose judgment on my father.

Fifteen years earlier, when I was in college, I had sought justice. I'd told Blount that Dad had molested me. But he'd told me that my dream about the camping trip was nothing more than a homosexual fantasy. At the time, psychologists knew little about homosexuality and even less about pedophilia. They were often lumped together under the category of perversion. I remember Blount's telling me when I was sixteen not only about the gay choirmaster who'd been run out of town but also about some scout leaders, exiled for molesting boys. My father had been instrumental in their banishment. I'm sure Blount imparted this to me in his attempts to cure me of homosexuality, but what I thought he meant was this: Your father is a hypocrite. But he is also a powerful man in this town. We are playing with dynamite here. Let's concentrate instead on making you heterosexual.

Now the world had changed. Dad was still a man of stature, but here he was, answering at last for his deeds. Ashwood had seen to that. And because of his threat, I could finally exercise the prerogative I had been unable to all of my life. I knew that whatever I said today in this conference would decide my father's future. Dad told me later that he'd felt a deep, searing sting in his leg. The pain had raced inside him, into his consciousness. No one in the room had noticed. He'd accepted the pain. He'd embraced it. He'd yearned for more. He told me that he had hoped he was having a heart attack.

We sat silently in Hahn's office, waiting for Dad's answer. He seemed to be liquefying inside. Although I didn't dwell on the thought, I knew that deep within me I still felt like protecting him. This wasn't because I loved him so much. The reason was something else: something had gone awry with my own sense of being. In a way I couldn't express to myself at the time, I felt like I *was* Dad. If he was going to be castrated, so was I. It was a thought both romantic and horrible.

Suddenly, Dad brightened, as if he had finally found permission to destroy or save himself. "Okay. Let's do it. Let's get it over with. But it will have to be done out of town."

"I'll find a surgeon and make the arrangements," Hahn said as he stretched and stood up from his chair. "And so you won't have to worry any more about Mister Ashwood, I'll call him myself. I'll get him off your back." Hahn offered his hand to Dad, who shook it without hesitation.

We left the office like executioners slipping out the back door of a prison. We cast our eyes about to see if anyone recognized us. Prepared to offer various excuses for our presence, we were also determined, all of us, I'm certain, not to think any further about what we had just done.

It did not occur to me that this was the first time that the four of us had been together to discuss anything so personal, so important, so real.

5

According to Dr. Linda Miles, a psychologist my father saw after his tenure with Hahn, my father's earliest memories were of the habitual trips he took with his mother to the old city cemetery to mourn for her first son, who had died of dysentery at the age of twenty-two months. The graveyard is cloistered within a wrought-iron fence and thick growths of wisteria. Today its perimeter is well illuminated by streetlights, but the interior remains dark and lush with aged camellias and crumbling monuments. One marks the grave where my father's mother often knelt in her black dress, wailing. My father remembered her as a stark figure twisting by the headstone in agony. Every time they traveled to the cemetery, she wept convulsively. "Can't you see he's an angel?" she would ask. But he could see nothing.

During the prolonged, loss of his mother's comfort, he waited without understanding, waited again and again and again, hurting, holding his hands to his ears against her sobbing. The edges of her form seemed to dissolve as she disappeared into the chilled intensity around her. The springy green grass touched his feet. He closed his eyes and grinned. There, standing in the air and smiling back, was his magnificent little brother. Young Walter leaned forward and gave the shining child a kiss, and the emptiness and pain flooded away from his body.

My father grew up on a place his mother called "Dream Hill"; it occupied half a city block next to the main crossroad of Tallahassee. Pathways connected the small Greek Revival house to a servants' quarters, vegetable garden, and three-horse stable of rough-sawn timber. Although the de Millys were successful cotton brokers before the Civil War, the family never accumulated any wealth. Walter's father, Charles, led a quiet life both as tax collector and the town's only insurance broker. He rarely spoke of his noble French ancestry or his forefather the governor, or even of his own father, who died, according to the obituarist, as the most beloved and generous man in the city, known as someone who would give money to people who could not afford to pay their property taxes.

Charles had copied his father's life. He joined the insurance business and ran it. He received a lifetime appointment as county tax collector. He gave money to the unfortunate. But sometimes, with no explanation, the hollow-cheeked Charles de Milly would decamp from his family and business, lock himself in his bedroom, and drink. He would respond to neither the pleas of his wife nor those of his children. He would remain confined for days on end. When the binge passed, he'd appear for breakfast as if nothing had happened. My father would look up from his plate of eggs and bacon, hoping to meet his father's eyes, yearning for a smile, a wink, any signal of love.

"Morning, Daddy," my father would say, but Charles de Milly, bathed in a dim light of humiliation, only looked down at the table.

As my father grew up, he found ways to escape the gloom. Like other boys of his time, he had a pet billy goat that would pull him around town in a carriage. Sometimes he and his buddies would take off into the surrounding woods. Miles to the south, the boys would explore the springs and caverns of old Florida. In the middle of nowhere they discovered Black Sink, so huge and deep that it was rumored to have no bottom. Only the bravest boys would grab the rope swing under an old oak tree and leap into the dark water far below.

The family spent the summers at the beach. When my father was thirteen, he built a sailboat there. Whenever he could, he fished or explored the sandy offshore islands a few miles to the west. It became a full life for Walter Junior and, for the most part, a life away from his father.

All the boys who spent their summers at the beach loved the water, but for Dad the water meant more than something to love. It was a salvation. Dad took every opportunity to stay away from home. He hated having a drunk for a father. He felt ashamed and angry, helpless to do anything to correct his situation. That's why I think he didn't care very much when, late in the afternoon out on the water, the wind would peter out, leaving him hours from shore. I think he treasured those times.

But as he came of age, his desire to be a part of his community called him back to Tallahassee. When he grew up and served on a church committee or raised money for a charity, the adoration and honor he received reinforced his self-image of a strong and moral man. He championed positive thinking and the belief that he could conquer temptation through will and prayer.

He had devised his philosophy not only because he was determined to avoid the path taken by his father but because he needed to conquer other temptations, very secret temptations that appeared with puberty. In the beginning, he hardly knew that his desires were perverted. He simply wanted what he saw. And what he saw, and surrendered to, was a nude photograph of his brother who had died at the age of twenty-two months. The town photographer had snapped it, and it was innocent enough in its gilded frame. But my father eyed the boy's buttocks. He wanted to feel them. He touched the oval glass. He imagined what it was like to press his fingers inside the child's little crack. Unable to let go of the boy's image, and despite his internal resistances, despite the voice within that said this is bad, my father returned to behold the photograph again and again.

My father's pedophilic impulses eventually convinced him that he was harboring evil thoughts. Although he tried to make himself forget the beauty of little boys, he knew that some day he would have to touch them. The first time it happened, he was fourteen. He called a neighborhood boy to come play in the woods. Dad made the child, who was only six, take his drawers off. Dad held the boy's penis for a moment and then, fearing what might happen if he were caught, instructed the boy to dress and not to tell anyone. Dad told himself he'd never do it again.

Determined to rise above his temptations, Dad went regularly to church, but what he learned gnawed at him. He couldn't keep the words of Jesus out of his mind. His minister had included them in a sermon once, on Children's Sunday. "But who so shall offend one of these little ones which believe in me, it were better for him that a millstone were hanged about his neck, and that he were drowned in the depth of the sea."

Dad was ashamed of his thoughts but decided that, if he prayed hard and spent his time doing good things for his community, God would enter his heart and rid him of the abominable desires. There were times when he believed this had happened. There were times when he was able to completely forget about his perversion, when he quite consciously loved himself, when he knew he was a very fine and honorable young man.

Yet, by the time he reached young adulthood, the feelings came so often that he was convinced that he was depraved, or worse. While everybody saw him as a real man, he knew he wasn't. And as long as he stayed in Tallahassee and sold insurance, he might never become one. He thought of running away. Sometimes he went into the dark and touched the world of suicide, never to follow through.

The Japanese bombed Pearl Harbor. He saw military service as a kind of trial. He got himself commissioned, and soon he was standing on the aft deck of a ship headed out of San Francisco en route to India.

The other sailors had gone to mess, but my father wasn't hungry. He walked aft alone. The huge propellers churned below him, shook the deck, and the chilly sea slipped away. He leaned his weight against the railing. Night set in. The glow over San Francisco shrank to a dim, distant blur. He looked at the roiling glow of the water. He wanted to jump. The propeller wash would suck him down. It wouldn't take long to die.

But Dad stopped himself. He bowed his head. God, if I do not come back from this war a changed man, I do not want to come back at all. He opened his eyes again and scanned the ocean. He knew that a man has no right telling God such things, even if it is done in earnest.

After the war he returned to Tallahassee to claim his family's tradition of civic duty and leadership. A group of businessmen offered him a position at a new bank, and he sold the family insurance agency. Business duties and meetings soon took his allegiance. His new responsibilities constantly distracted him. He was praised for his spirited resourcefulness and high principles. In time, one of the town's most prominent men approached Dad and asked him to form a new Boy Scout troop. Dad said he'd think about it. He knew his sexual inclinations could remain a secret and under control. It wasn't such a weighty problem, anyway. He dismissed his concerns and agreed to do it. Within a month the sons of Tallahassee's old guard had joined his new troop. Soon the whole group was trekking to the woods and camping out nearly every weekend.

My mother tells me that she had dated a few young men before Dad, but none measured up. She met him at a wedding. He was thirty-four and available.

"I fell in love," she said, "but it wasn't easy dating him. The old ladies of Tallahassee tried to discourage me. Other, perfectly acceptable girls had already given up on him. The old ladies of Tallahassee would stop me on the street. They'd say, 'You're wasting your time chasing after Walter de Milly. He's a confirmed bachelor.'" Mother pretended shock. "I ignored them," she said.

I knew what the women meant, even if Mother didn't. In 1950 "confirmed bachelor" was a polite way to characterize a man who might be one of those: a man with no interest in women. Proper ladies would never explain or, mostly likely, even *think* further.

For two years my mother patiently stayed put while Dad took his scout troop camping. But she still managed to date him, even when Dad's mother made her disapproval known. Mother says that the woman was jealous and possessive. Mrs. de Milly would find whatever excuses she could to interfere, often by insisting that she accompany the couple on their dates. "When we took drives in the country, she would sit in the back seat," Mother said. She described Mrs. de Milly as leaning more forward than upright, eyes electric, chattering gleefully, changing subjects whenever my mother tried to talk.

Nevertheless, my mother was in love, and she knew that my father must sooner or later make a decision to break away from his mother. Eventually, it happened. "When your father made the announcement to his mother that we were going to marry," my mother said, "her face fell in disbelief. Do you know what she told Walter later on? She said, 'Mary has blue eyes. There are enough blue eyes in the de Milly family.' Can you imagine?" Mother laughs when she repeats this story, but sometimes I see the hurt.

Despite the obstacles, my parents were married in May 1950. By the fourth year my sister and I had arrived.

6

APRIL 1956 AT SIX O'CLOCK ON A SPRING MORNING IN THE THIRD
year of little Walt's life, his dad awakes. He rises, knowing what he wants
to do. He will take his son on an outing. He puts on his khaki slacks and
hiking boots, walks into the den, and finds Walt. "We're going exploring
today," says Walter, picking Walt up by his arms.

Walt hangs limp, head back, chin nudged against his father's tummy,
grinning. His mother gives them a breakfast of bacon and eggs. Father and
son soon disappear into the shady woodlands where Walter once played
as a child. Walt rides on his father's shoulders. The boy's legs clasp his
father's neck. Walter moves along handsomely, hiking at a steady cadence
along the old dirt trail. Walt leans sideways beneath an outstretched tree
limb, unafraid of falling. Walter holds his son's legs snugly. He beats down
the brush. Walt feels his father's strength and sureness. From his perch the
boy feels heroic. He chatters about bears, nodding, nodding, as his father
hikes. It feels like they're breathing together.

They reach the lip of Black Sink, where Walter stops. "It's bottomless,"
Walter tells his son. The boy hears the echoes of water dripping into
the abyss.

They are tiny figures against the spectacle. The trees here are relics.
They're always dying and dropping rotten limbs, but they seem never
to thoroughly die. They lean inward and form a shroud over a deep
circular well in the earth two hundred feet across. Drooping ferns and
dead leaves veil its walls, which plunge vertically to unknown depths.
Along the descent, orchids with tiny red blooms cling to a crag and then,
at the point where all light seems to disappear, the shaft of a dead tree
vanishes into a body of anthracite water.

Walter takes his son from his shoulders. He squeezes Walt tightly, in
a familiar, insistent rhythm that the child finds both incomprehensible

and distressing. With a stilted smile Walter slips his hand beneath the boy's rompers and cups his hand over the child's penis. It feels good to the boy. Walt watches the fluttering canopy of oak leaves and the cool sky. He sees his father's privileged blue eyes, like crystals of ice, melting over him.

Walter rubs the boy. He rubs hard, unforgivingly. He pulls the boy's pants down to his knees. He wiggles his finger into his son's bottom. It hurts. Walter has done this before but not so deeply. Walt kicks, but his father doesn't care. Walter pushes his finger in.

"No," Walt says, whining. His hair lies against his father's forearm. His eyes plead. He arches himself backward, pushing, straining to break away.

"Be quiet," the father commands, as if he's giving his son a bath. "Hold still."

Walt lifts his eyes to meet his father's, but the man is furious, not angry but furious, as if he can't find what he's looking for. What have I done wrong? the boy wonders. Walter grasps his son's penis and slips his other hand behind the boy. The boy squirms, but his father holds him tighter. Now the boy turns his head sideways.

"Hold still," the agitated father says. Around them the only sound is the plinking of water below. Walter hurts the boy. The child pushes his head back, wincing, then sideways again. He imagines with all his might that he can thrust himself out of Daddy's arms and into Black Sink. He shuts out the world in a timeless, hypnotic blink. For the father there is no son, no unconditional love, only unblemished skin, soft, delicious, like syrup on a biscuit. The father swells with euphoria, standing in the moldering leaves with his son cradled in his arms. The father hasn't the faintest idea that he's holding a son who isn't there.

Walt is far away, in the company of serpents, long shards of glass, planets, messengers dressed in suits, and paintings that could come alive. There's a paddle fan, a workshop, a cemetery, a hospital room, a diamond floating on the water, and the underside of a table once used by King Arthur, where the boy scribbles desperately with a crayon. Only his skin experiences the pulling and stretching, the devastating, ravaging adoration of his father's hands.

The father is in his own trance, his eyes riveted on his son's body. His fantasies are coming true. Walter has his very own boy. He holds Walt with one hand and reaches a peak with the other.

Then, carefully wiping himself off, he comes back to his world. He puts his son's clothes back together and carries him through the forest toward the car. He carries the boy silently, marching toward civilization.

When Dad drove us away from the forest, the imperfect, incomplete, brand-new Walt sat in the front seat with the wind blowing against his cheeks. I had just come into being, but I didn't feel new. I had merely stepped into a familiar body, a life I already knew.

I watched a stand of trees flicker past us. I wanted to cry, but I didn't know why. I was sad about the whole world. I did not understand that another Walt had disappeared and that he would remain a secret, even from me.

When Dad and I came home from the woods and I saw my mother standing in the kitchen, I stopped short, swept dizzy by dejà vu. She certainly knew who I was. When I hugged her, she felt familiar but unreal. I wondered if she had the wrong boy. She handed me an oatmeal cookie, then wiped the crumbs from my mouth.

A week later my father called to me from his old chair. "Come here," he said. He pulled me into his lap. I picked at the brass studs along the arm and ran my fingers across a crack in the leather. His fingers found my tummy and I shuddered. "Did you know that God sacrificed his only begotten son, who descended into Hell for three days, and then rose from the dead?"

"What's Hell?" I asked.

"A bad, bad place. It's where the Devil lives and a fire that never goes out. It is where people go when they are bad and don't believe in God. They burn forever."

Then his eyes brightened. "This is my son, with whom I am well pleased," he pronounced, smiling.

I must be Christ, I think. Someone is dead and I'm Christ instead.

I heard a voice. I saw a boy and chased him. We ran down a dirt road. Then I thought that it was just a memory and there was no boy. But it is a boy, I think. It is. He's my brother.

"Mommy, Mommy," I said, tugging at her dress, "do I have a twin brother?"

"No, honey," she said in an amused tone. "Where'd you get that idea?"

"I don't know," I answered, "you're sure? You don't remember him?"

"Yes, son," she said lovingly, "I'm sure. You're the only son I have, and I love you!"

"I love you too, Mommy," I said, disappointed. Mommy's lying. I know about the other boy. We played together.

Then she said, "Honey, let me look at your hair."

She held my light blond hair in her fingers, looking at the roots.

She called to Dad. "Walter!"

"What?"

"Come look at Walt."

Dad came over and Mother held a lock of my hair out so he could see. I stood beneath them and didn't move. I wondered if I ought to be hurting.

"Look at what's happening," she said. "Look at the roots."

"They're dark," he said.

"Why, isn't that something?" she wondered aloud. "He's becoming a brunette."

My new hair grew in quickly. It would never change back.

Whenever Dad appeared, the other Walt came out to take my place. Dad didn't even have to touch me. Sometimes all it would take to switch was the sound of the front door cracking open or the rattle of the newspaper as Dad put it down. When these things happened, I toppled like a tower of building blocks. The first Walt fell, and the second materialized.

Sometimes, though, we both awoke together. As I got older, this happened often, usually when the whole family was around. By the time I was eight, Dad had begun quick morning devotionals at the breakfast table. He'd take the Bible from its place on the kitchen counter and sit next to me.

"I'm going to read from the General Epistle of James," he said, slipping on his black glasses. " 'Wherefore, my beloved brethren, let every man be swift to hear, slow to speak, slow to wrath.' " He put the palm of his hand on the page.

"Do you know what that means?" he asked me.

"To be patient and listen," I said.

"That's right," Dad said.

"And don't get angry," said Caroline, "that's what wrath is."

"That's right," Dad said. "Wrath is anger." He reached under the table and put his hand on my penis. He squeezed. He squeezed again. Both Walts remained awake. After Dad closed the Bible, he looked at Mother and nodded. She began her prayer. I poured myself into her, I closed my eyes tight, I drank her verdant words: ". . . and Jesus, who loves Caroline and Walt so very much, look upon them today, protect them from the cold . . ."

Afterward, she smiled. Dad kept his hand on my crotch.

"Walt's going to win his race today!" Dad exclaimed.

I grinned. My lips moved. "Yeah," I said. "I'm going to stomp 'em."

Dad beamed. "Jack be nimble, Jack be quick . . . " He pressed his hand on my dick.

I smiled and chatted. But amnesia trailed me like a shadow, covering what my eye could not see. I could have carried on a conversation while someone was sawing off my leg.

Even if the other Walt hadn't taken over the experience beneath the table, I would have been too humiliated to expose Dad. A boy is not going to spill his sexual embarrassment before his mother and sister. Even if I'd been brave enough to do it, I knew no one would have believed me. Dad would have laughed if I had complained.

I can hear him. He'd tell Mother: "I'm tickling him."

"Stop it, honey," she'd complain, "not at the table."

The relentless advances by Dad and the constant switching between my selves affected my ability to concentrate. Life held no continuity. I tried to hide my confusion, even from myself. My favorite ploy was to be silly. In class I became a cut-up. In the second grade, when I was seven, I sat by Jimmy Ogden, crouching low behind the girl in front of me, puckering my mouth like a fish and rolling my eyes back.

Mrs. Harris, my teacher, saw me. "When Walt is ready to pay attention," she told to the class, "we'll continue."

I froze in delight, humiliation, terror. I immediately wanted to do anything to make up for my badness. But I could do nothing other than make sure I remained watchful of Mrs. Harris. At the lunch break, I walked up to her, nearly in tears. "I'm sorry," I said.

"You must learn to pay attention to me," she said. "Now go on to lunch, and I'll forget that it happened."

Since I couldn't always be silly in class, I checked out. It happened often, especially if Dad had handled me too much that morning.

During the first weeks of the third grade my teacher, Mrs. Taggard, thought I was retarded. I thought she didn't like me. She stared at me with her egg-white eyes and I stared back.

"Walt," she would say, pointing to a succession of planets she'd strung across the room, "how many planets are there?"

"Nine," I said from my trance.

"Well, that's right," she said, suspiciously. The thing is, she had made a mistake. She had transposed Venus and Mars. I wondered what the point was in telling her. She was the one who was stupid.

She called my mother to tell her that I was either dumb or lazy. Mother tells me that she couldn't help but wonder whether Mrs. Taggard was right. Mother knew I was bright, but she also knew I was a quiet seven-year-old. She wrestled with the thought that perhaps I had some defect that was visible only in other contexts, away from the protection of home. Mother wondered for months, watching me, distressed that the future might not unfold with kindness, fearing that some inadequacy would eventually confine me, or her. There were times, she noticed, when I didn't seem right. It wasn't that I seemed dumb or slow but that I sparkled or faltered without reason or cause. My friends and I would play in the backyard, screaming and giggling. The next moment, I'd withdraw without explanation to my room, where I'd lie awake in bed. Every child is different, she told herself.

At the end of the year, when I was eight, Mrs. Taggard called Mother to come in for a conference to discuss the IQ test results that had just come back. Pointing to a mark on the extreme right of the bell curve, she told my mother that I could do whatever I wanted in life. My mother, having been taught politeness in all circumstances of life, accepted the teacher's report graciously, and the smile she gave was not so much one of relief but of happiness. Mother was delighted that I was nearly through with my schooling under Mrs. Taggard.

One summer at the beach, when I was nine, I had to learn to keep secrets both to protect my friends and to protect myself from becoming aware of what Dad did to them. I would, by some merciful feat, manage to forget—if not the whole memory of a crime, at least the text of it, the "memory" itself. I can see now, rather clearly, one such afternoon of bubble gum and shattered hope. The first clue that something very wrong had happened came at nap time. I couldn't sleep. The rest of my family, stripped down to their underwear because of the heat, slept in their rooms. I knelt on a dark green army trunk in my bedroom and looked out my window. Fear, loneliness, and sorrow filled me. I did not understand. The pain held me in the chest, burning, the way cold air burns the lungs. It felt as if it were coming from a place inside me, a place I ought to be able to see. It hurt so much that it seemed to have a voice. I knew the pain must have come for a reason, but whatever the reason was, I didn't understand. Nothing around me was wrong, but everything felt hopeless. I didn't know what to do. I stared out the window and told myself I wasn't going to think about it any more.

The gray clouds of a squall crouched to the west. Darkening, growing, the storm approached us. On the horizon whitecaps rose, rolled along a ways, then spilled over themselves in thin white ribbons. The clouds composed new heavy shapes that were coming closer, casting a steel-gray rain curtain wide across the sea. I pressed my nose against the window screen and smelled the cool, keen air. Suddenly, a gust of wind chased the cold rain through the window, stinging my face.

I imagined another world, a planet at war. All around the earth nuclear bombs were exploding, annihilating humanity. I'd run down to the water and swim under the surface, waiting until the radiation passed. I could hold my breath for hours. Now I imagined myself a lord of the sea, swimming, streaking miles offshore, tumbling in the din, streamlined, clutching dolphins, piercing the surf, shrieking, the last boy, the most fearless boy on earth in 1962.

I sighed. The pain clung to my insides. I'm not going to think about it.

The storm hung over us. I imagined myself running outside in the rain, darting into the sea, drowning. No. I hoped to be struck by lightning, right there in the bunk.

The rain passed. I went out to the front porch. Mother, wearing a white cotton dress and holding a white towel, wiped the water off a rocking chair. She sat down with a magazine. I sat next to her. I listened to the water dripping from the roof and into the sand around the house, tap-tap-tapping like nervous fingers on a desk. I listened to Mother's breathing. I felt her softness, her pure and merciful warmth. I knew I loved her. Dad came out with a broom. He was still wearing his underwear. I knew he'd slept because his hair was all frowzy. I laughed. He made a silly, ferocious face and began sweeping the water off the porch floor. Caroline came out with one of her Nancy Drew books. We each seemed lost in a tranquil state and uttered not a word. Around us, the copper porch screens snapped in the wind.

I couldn't stand the silence any longer. I ran down the sand dune and looked at the water. There was nothing but our boat anchored about a hundred yards out. Suddenly, I had an idea and hollered up to Mother.

"Look at the reef!" I yelled, pointing rigidly to the sea. "There's a big ship wrecked!"

Mother stood up, eyes wide open, aghast, looking at me and then to the empty horizon and back. She walked outside, squinting in the sun. Caroline stood up too and saw nothing, looked at me, and scrunched her face as if she thought I was crazy. Dad sat in his chair, at first impassive, then alert.

"Where is it?" my mother asked, "where?"

I collapsed in the sand howling. Caroline laughed, and Dad, as if suddenly aware that something funny had happened, let out a "Ha!" Mother, mouth open, eyed me firmly, stood with arms akimbo, and pretended disgust. I was delighted.

I looked around, thinking of what to do next. I wanted Dad to come play with me out in the water, maybe take me in the boat somewhere. I watched it for a moment. Empty, it tugged lethargically against the anchor line, rising and falling over unhurried waves. I ran farther down to the beach and stepped in the water, my eyes fixed on the boat. All was still. The image brightened abruptly. I stepped back, hurting, pain falling around me.

I did not remember the day before, much less how it was causing my pain. What I know now is that my friend Douglas had been visiting me. It had been bright and hot, and we had gone down to the water to swim. Dad had followed. Douglas and I were taking turns standing on Dad's shoulders and leaping into the water. Douglas wasn't used to being around the water. When he began screaming, I thought he'd stepped on something harmless. Maybe a crab had pinched him.

"What's wrong?" I asked.

"A jellyfish stung me," he said, wincing.

Big deal, I thought. They had never hurt me. Douglas was my age, but he was more slimly built. He could whistle between his teeth. I thought it was a very masculine skill, and I admired him for it.

Douglas bent over, holding himself. Dad waded hurriedly toward him.

"Where'd you get stung?" Dad asked, his eyes alive.

"On my dick," Douglas whispered. "It hurts!"

Dad became silken. "Go out to the boat," he said. Dad followed behind Douglas. Because the boat was anchored in deeper water, they had to swim to reach it. Douglas climbed aboard, then Dad. I swam out alongside the boat, wanting to see. Douglas stood near the stern, half-hidden by the cockpit, and pulled his baggy shorts down. Dad went to the forward cabin and brought something out. He sat next to Douglas. I pulled myself up over the gunwale so I could see into the boat. With one forearm Dad struck sweat from his brow, while his other arm rested on Douglas's thigh. Dad had Douglas's penis between thumb and fingers. Douglas grimaced, stared at his own penis, stared at Dad's hand, stared in shock. It seemed that the picture he saw was both mesmerizing and horrible. He had been crying. His tears sparkled in the sunlight.

"What are you doing?" I asked. I tried to see better but I couldn't.

"Just putting suntan lotion on it," Dad said, keeping firmly to his position. I could tell he was irritated at me. He had the determined and furious expression I'd seen so many times before when I'd tried to push his hands away from me.

"Suntan lotion?" I asked. "Why?"

"Because that'll make it feel better," Dad snarled. "You stay away while I finish." I let go and treaded water, watching Dad lean over Douglas. I knew that suntan lotion wouldn't make Douglas feel better. I knew that Dad could make up his own reasons for the things he did. I turned around toward the beach cabin. Caroline was coming down the path through the sea oats. She was looking toward us. She waded into the water and began to swim out. I waited for Dad to let go of Douglas. I wanted him to finish before Caroline reached us, but his desperation intensified even as she swam closer.

She came over to me. "What are they doing?"

"Douglas got stung by a jellyfish," I said. "Dad's rubbing suntan lotion on him."

She paused and looked at the boat. "Why's he taking so long?"

"I don't know." I didn't know what to do. I felt guilty. Daddy, we're doing something wrong. Quit it, Daddy. Quit it. But he wouldn't quit. I knew that this was all my fault. I should have warned Douglas. I shouldn't have invited him down. Besides, Daddy wasn't supposed to do that with anyone else but me. I spread my palms, sliced the water at my neck, and watched, waiting, still, like an alligator eyes his prey.

A new Walt, the observing Walt, ascended to consciousness. He didn't want anyone, not Douglas, not Caroline, not me, not anyone, to know what Mr. de Milly was really like. This Walt didn't want Caroline running back to Mother and telling her that our father was playing with Douglas's penis. If Mother knew what our father was doing, she might ask Walt if he'd ever done that same thing with him. This Walt couldn't risk that. He swam in circles around the boat. He looked back at his father and saw the trance in the man's eyes. Caroline held her head above the water and examined the boat. Walt hoped she would think that their father was just putting a bandage on Douglas or checking for welts left by the jellyfish. But Walt could tell that she was already angry. She pushed through the water. She glared at the boat. She grimaced like she was going to cry. Walt knew she hated it when their father paid too much attention to their friends. She hated it when he put their friends on his lap and hugged them until they squirmed away.

Walt hated this. He stopped swimming, closed his eyes, and sank under the water. He blushed, he burned hot as a sun. He disappeared. I'm the one joined to Dad. We are the beast.

Suddenly, I popped to the surface. I became detached from myself, floating above my body. "Let's go back up," Caroline said in an undisturbed tone. "It's lunchtime."

I swam to shore, half numb, unaware of sensations. I looked back into the water. Caroline was following me. She looked like she was swimming through a mist. I neither saw the boat nor looked for it. I saw my figure below me, foreshortened, neck bared to the sky. I walked up the dune to the house, my head bowed down, staring down the white sand. It crunched. In front of me a furious red wasp flapped its wings.

I went into the beach house and took a shower. I could hear Caroline and then Douglas and Dad coming up through the side door. When I was almost through showering, Dad came into the bathroom and took off his swimsuit. His penis was hard. He took the soap from its dish and began rubbing his chest with it. I stood next to him, rinsing myself. Suddenly, without thought or determination, I came back into my body and hit him hard on his back. Dad laughed. I bolted from the shower, dripping water on the tile floor.

"Stand on the mat," he ordered from the shower.

"No," I said, confused at what I'd done. I grabbed a towel and went to my bedroom. I put on a pair of shorts. Dad finished his shower. He came into my bedroom, towel wrapped around his waist.

"Bend over," he said.

"Why?" I asked, afraid.

"Don't stand on the bathroom floor dripping water all over it," he said. "Your mother's told you not do that. Now bend over."

I turned away from him and put my hands on my knees. He spanked me, hard. He hit me again. I didn't cry.

"What's going on?" my mother asked from the front porch.

"Walt's being bad," Dad said, "messing up the house."

Mother didn't say anything. The world around me was dark. I could see the beach house below me again. On our porch screen I could see the slightly real arc of a smile and, farther down, the sea biting the shore.

The spankings I received from my father usually occurred when I had caused my mother some distress. As I look back, I see that his anger was usually justified. But I often sensed multiple meanings. If he spanked me for slopping water all over the floor, he was also punishing me for interfering with—or making too uncomfortably real—his boy-loving. If he spanked me for getting muddy from wrestling with my friend in the backyard, he was also punishing me for having passion for someone else.

The physical punishments were not in themselves what I would consider abuse. But the messages kept me shattered. They drove the machinery that kept secrets, told lies, kept track of who remembered what, and which truths would be told to whom.

By the time I was ten and finishing the fifth grade, Dad had found new ways to obtain his pleasures. One school morning he walked into my room, leaned over my bed, placed the palm of his hand on my penis, and squeezed it, waking me up. I opened my eyes and there he was, stopped in time, smiling down at me. All I could think of was my erect penis under the sheets. I pretended to ignore his gesture.

The next morning, while I was still asleep, Dad came in for another try. This time, it wasn't me who opened his eyes. The boy that so fiercely glared at his father was a devil.

"Time to get up," his dad said, grinning, tall and crisp in his white oxford shirt.

Walt blazed back. He did not speak. His hands lay still and dead beneath the sheets. His father waited, as if to elicit a grunt from the boy. But the boy only burned. His father laughed, an innocent, surprised, infectious laugh, his way of telling Walt that as far as he was concerned, nothing was wrong.

The father left the room as if nothing had happened. Walt lay there, his muscles taut and scorching, hating himself, hating bitter life. Quickly, he plunged back into the regions of nothingness.

Although I once believed I had a twin brother who died, that idea got lost, or transformed. By the end of the sixth grade I was intractably haunted by the sense that something was very wrong with me. The sensations flickered behind my thoughts, evading direct observation. I knew there was more to the world than I could see, and I knew that it was very wrong. In occasional flashes of comprehension, I sensed the presence of evil, and I feared—I knew—it was somewhere within me.

In the same way a blind person is gifted with a heightened auditory capacity, I enjoyed a measure of cold intelligence. I was compelled to analyze the world, nature, life, the human body. I wanted to understand what made us work, what was inside us. As I walked through the barren landscape around me, I regarded not what was absent but what was left. It was an interminable journey, taken according to a kind of preexisting hieroglyphic knowledge that I translated on the fly.

I wasn't always alone. Ray, a friend who lived down the street from us, was gifted in science and led me into any number of explorations and projects. Both of us had erector sets and racetracks. During the summers we put them together, making enormous constructions. We built mazes out of refrigerator boxes and designed computers using Christmas lights and aluminum foil. As we grew and became more proficient, we learned electronics. We built power supplies and amplifiers and sirens that could scream across the neighborhood. We had chemistry sets, we studied insects under microscopes, and we set off explosions.

One humid summer afternoon we built a huge papier-mâché landscape for our racetrack. Two days later we noticed a maggot-green fuzz had spread up and down the little mountainsides. We forgot about the racetrack itself. Every day after that, as soon as we got home from school, we rushed to our experiment, hoping to find new varieties of growth.

We studied the molds with the greatest curiosity, comparing the horrible looking, hairy outbreaks to photographs in a science book. The whole monstrous thing became revolting to look at, especially to my friend's mother. One day, when in our gleeful opinion it reached its peak of grossness and began to produce vile smells, she made us throw it out.

At home I began to study the workings of the human body. This got the attention of my mother and a doctor friend, who recommended that I read *Gray's Anatomy*. I concentrated on the cardiovascular system, memorizing the names of every artery and vein in the human body. I learned the physiology of the heart. My doctor, who had become accustomed to my anatomical questions, suggested in a moment of inspiration that my mother ought to bring me a cow's heart so I could examine it. My mother made the request to a butcher, who provided the organ. With my anatomy book open before me and Ray at my side, I dissected the heart, proudly pointing out the anatomical features. I wrote a report about it for my sixth-grade science class. It was as if I was looking into my own heart. Something was wrong with mine, something elusive and relentless and ever present no matter how much I tried to forget the feeling.

Sometimes, I watched Dad. All the contentment in the world belonged to him and none to me. I thought it was because I was doing something wrong. I watched him, I loved him. Sometimes I felt that we should go mad together. Even so, I hushed that idea. The truth is, my awe of life was irrepressible. My curiosity made me reluctant to challenge my outer world, for I was too busy trying to understand it. I was, by all appearances, a happy, bright, and well-behaved child. Everyone who knew me expected me to grow up to be a resourceful, kind, and loving gentleman, just like my dad. Not even he thought otherwise.

7

IN THE FALL OF 1964 I WAS ONLY TEN, NOT YET OLD ENOUGH TO JOIN the scouts, but Dad decided it would be a good idea to take me on a camping trip with them. It may not make sense that I wanted to be in his company, but I did. The everyday Walt adored Dad and would go anywhere with him. At that point in my life, the other Walts—the peaceful sleeping infant, the terrified observer, the furious child-beast—kept all the knowledge of the Bad Father to themselves. There was no incest between the Good Father and me. The Good Father had no evil. What made me feel better than anything was watching someone else melt in the presence of his magic power. Of course, no one genuflected before Dad, but in my eyes they did. I filled myself with the certainty that I was not only well protected but invincible.

On the afternoon of the camping trip our group—five other boys and six other scout masters, met at the edge of Silver Lake. Dad stood splendidly before us in his khaki-green uniform and gathered us around him. "Don't leave the trail," he instructed. We set out to hike, threading our way through the tall gray cypress trees and around their curious, deformed knees, which curl into the water. I carried a backpack and the new sleeping bag Mother had given me. I followed behind Dad. We moved along in the shadows. Now and then a boy yelled or sprang a branch into another's face. The lake echoed back, calling, snapping, squishing. We noticed a stench in the air. Off to our left by a fallen tree we heard the buzz of flies. We saw a dead puppy, white and black, his nose caked in dried blood. The boys crowded around it. One of them picked up a stick and poked the dog's swollen tummy.

Dad came upon us and said to leave it alone. I wanted to stay. The other boys walked on, but I bent over the puppy, hoping to find something, anything more, a clue, a name tag, a memory. There was nothing. I ran to catch up with the rest.

It was dark and so wet that the ground foamed beneath our shoes. Dad warned us to be careful not to trip over logs or step on water moccasins. Late in the afternoon we reached the drier soil of the campsite. While the other men dispersed, Dad unfolded a thick green canvas tent. It smelled of old smoke, just like Dad did whenever he'd come home from his other camping trips. I held a corner of the tent while he pitched it.

The boys made a campfire. After the wood burned down to coals, they cooked hamburgers. It was late when I finally got to eat mine. When we'd all finished, Dad told me to wash my plate with water from a canteen. Then he told me to go to bed. I crawled inside the tent and into my sleeping bag. I zipped it up snugly and put my head down on the red felt lining.

I could hear muffled voices, a few scouts stirring the campfire with pine sticks, tossing in more wood. Above them rose my dad's gentle voice. Now and then they laughed. Dad was telling a story. I tried to sleep but couldn't. After what seemed like a hundred years, Dad concluded the evening.

"The day is done," he told the boys. "Don't stay up talking all night. Remember to put out the fire."

Dad reached his hand into our tent and yanked the flaps aside. He crawled in and unrolled his sleeping bag next to mine. I was on my back, still awake and listening to the noises outside. I turned on my side.

"Dad," I asked, "do you think there are bears out there?"

"Yes," he said, stripping down to his underwear. He slipped on his pajamas. "But they won't come near our camp. They can smell us and they don't like humans."

"How about wolves?" I pulled my sleeping bag up to my neck and watched Dad crawl into his.

"No, son," he answered, resting his head on his hands. "Foxes might approach the camp, but they're even more timid around humans than bears. And there'll be plenty of raccoons. They'll come sometime later in the night and try to get into our food." Dad smiled at me. Raccoons didn't scare me.

The voices outside faded. I closed my eyes and fell asleep. The puppy dog lies on his side. I yell to another boy and he runs over and picks up the puppy and . . . I'm taking a nap with Dad and he's holding me and the world feels good . . . pressing against me.

I opened my eyes in the darkness and smelled the tent. Oh, yeah, I thought, we're camping. Dad had unzipped my bag. He'd put his arm inside. It felt good, except I hoped he wouldn't touch me down there the way he did in the fallout shelter. I was sleepy. I drifted back into the night.

I woke again. I felt Dad's hand on my penis. I grabbed his wrist and moved it away.

I woke again. Dad had his hand around my penis. Take your hand away, I thought, leave me alone. I grabbed his hand and pulled it away. Just as quickly, he thrust his arm back. I knew what this meant. He wanted me to give up. He wanted to hold me there. I pulled my pajamas up high and turned on my side away from him, breathing fast. I was so tired.

I woke again, sweating, feeling something . . . Dad's fingers wrapped around my penis. I'm dreaming this, I thought. No, I'm awake.

"No," I whispered, sharply.

I tried to pull Dad off me, but he shoved my hand away. I tried again. He wouldn't let go. I grabbed him with both hands, but he was stronger and he held on. He stroked my penis.

I pretended to be asleep. The sensations grew. My penis was hard. I lay still for a moment. An unfamiliar, urgent pulse rushed inside me, tensing, heating. I was afraid to speak, afraid someone would hear us. I tried to see into the darkness. I had to pee. No, I thought. I tried to hold it back, but I couldn't stop, it felt so good. Dad's arm, rigid, moved faster. I wriggled. I tried to stop. He held me tighter and rubbed me, and it ached and burned and burned inside. I pulled the lining of my bag, I let go of a breath, I shuddered, dark and bright. Somewhere off in the woods I thought I heard two panthers cry.

Dad held my penis, softer now. I thought I had peed in my bag. I wanted to die. It was silent, black. The Walts tore through outer space. Burn us up, they pleaded, hurry and burn us up.

The floating Walt saw the camp below us and the boy lying in the tent. The child's lips were parted; his chest moved to the slow pitch of a numbing, impossible slumber. Next to him lay his father, who'd pulled his hand out of Walt's sleeping bag and moved it into his own.

There was light. I awoke. Dew had settled on the tent. The lining of my sleeping bag stuck to my body. The pine cones hurt. I was hot and felt tangled up in my bag. Then I felt faint. I looked for Dad, but he was gone.

I stepped outside the tent onto pine needles. Some of the grownups were getting a breakfast fire going. One man, knobby and hairy and naked, shaved with a straight razor in front of a little mirror hooked to a tree. He eyed me, swinging around just enough so that I could see his penis. It scared me. A man wearing underwear stood under a tarp pouring coffee out of a metal pot. The men were laughing. They looked at me. I stood there in my pajamas, numb, while the frightened Walt took over my consciousness.

Later, I found myself alone at the edge of the clearing where our camp was. Time had turned still. I stood looking at the bark of a tree, but I didn't know why, or how I'd gotten there. I breathed easily, but I felt as if I was gasping. I felt heat and tingling in my penis. I was alone, I wanted to be left alone. I didn't know why I felt this way. I saw Dad and the boys looking at something on the ground. When he squatted, they leaned against him, and he marked the air above the hoofprints of a deer.

The next day we returned home. My mother hugged me, and I smiled. I didn't know why I smiled.

"Did you have fun?" she asked, busily unpacking the ice chest.

"Yes." I leaned against the counter and untied my shoes. I threw my dirty socks on the floor.

She saw something in my eyes—a sparkle? Relieved, she turned to Dad and kissed him. I went to my room and lay down on my bed.

One night not long after this, when I was trying to sleep, I heard signals in my head, a drumming sound. It wasn't my heartbeat, but it had the same rhythm. Everything outside me was amplified, throbbing. I couldn't stand it. I lay very still.

The experience would come again, even when I was playing in the backyard or at school. It was at this time in my life that I realized for certain that I was different from everybody else. I didn't know exactly why, or how, but I knew that these strange sensations dancing through my consciousness were not normal. I had read about ESP, and this is how I came to think that perhaps I was receiving some sort of signals. Perhaps if I listened carefully, I could interpret them. Sometimes a voice seemed to drone on flatly in the background, like a long radio announcement. I could never quite make out the words, even though it went on and on. I eventually learned to ignore the voice or shove it to the background.

Sometimes I felt like I had forgotten how to know who I was. Thoughts came into my mind that felt like someone else's. I ignored them. I hated school. Everyone liked me, but I didn't want to be with anyone. I only wanted to be invisible. To get out of class I complained of sore throats. Sometimes my knees hurt. Maybe the doctors would find out what was wrong with me.

My mother took me to an internist, to an allergist, and to an orthopedic specialist. The first doctor found nothing. The second found allergens and prescribed weekly injections. The orthopedist found calcium deposits below my kneecaps. This fascinated me. Here was an opportunity for me to understand my body. I began studying the problem in the medical books my mother had given me months before. I memorized parts of the anatomy and the medical description of my condition, which I announced to my friends. "Osteochondrosis of the tuberosity of the tibia," I answered with rhythm and confidence whenever they asked why I couldn't participate in gym class. I learned that speaking precisely about my physical condition seemed to insulate me from too much prying, too much curiosity about my inner world. I lost myself in hobbies and avoided sports. Something about a gang of boys terrified me.

A few months after the camping trip by Silver Lake, I officially joined the Boy Scouts on my eleventh birthday. At the first meeting a boy took my hat away. I had to sing to the troop before they'd give it back. I went home crying. I gathered my courage, however, and soon began to focus on advancement in rank. I moved rapidly. While the other Boy Scouts played football on our camping trips, I worked on my merit badges, learning about citizenship, first aid, Indian lore, and safety.

I was growing. Lanky and dark haired, I swam quietly, politely, through a private sea of pain. I loved my mother and father and sister, but I also felt that they wouldn't love me if they knew my secrets, the strange sensations, the cruel voice inside me.

To those around me I appeared preoccupied. I worked doggedly on my Boy Scout badges. I read. I stared blankly into space. I looked at Dad as some kind of a god. He was handsome, and he loved me. He spent half his time at church meetings and Boy Scout meetings and going to the hospital and raising money for charity. He was a very good man—that was for sure.

My mother remembers the times when I could not hide the pain. She has told me that for my twelfth birthday, I had six or seven friends over. While they played in the backyard with Dad, I ran behind the fallout shelter and cried. My friends wanted to know what was wrong with me. No one knew. I wouldn't say. But the truth is that I was jealous of my dad's attention to my friends. I was just as in love with Dad as he was with me. I wanted him alone. My mother worried about me. She wondered if I was going through a phase.

In my gloom one morning as I dressed for school, I saw on my chest of drawers an index card that had been folded in half. It was a note from Dad, written in blue ink. He must have come into my room when I was still sleeping. "Son," it said, "my father taught me something which I'll never forget. It has helped me throughout my life. It may sound simple, but it is true. I pass it on to you with love: 'Smile, and the world smiles with you.' Remember this, son, and soon you'll discover how happy your world can be. Smile, and the world smiles with you! Love, Daddy."

I made sure no one was peeking into my bedroom, and I tried to smile. Somehow I would bridge the chasm; I would go to the other side where

I knew I would find comfort and peace. I went to school in a trance, but I smiled. I smiled through the winter, the spring, and the wicked silence of summer.

I did not see what I see now: after the camping trip at Silver Lake, Dad left me alone, forever. He could no longer expect me to lie with him as an innocent child ought to lie with his father. Yet my new freedom did not release me from anything. The pain lingered, pulsed, blistered. My soul, hollow and torn, lay abandoned somewhere in the forest. Dad continued to adore prepubescent boys, and I strained to find a way to the other side. In an effort to extricate myself from the pain, I eventually became expert at finding humor and silliness in everyday life. I made demented faces. If I was in class, I ignored my teacher and counted tiles on the ceiling. I pressed my fingers against my wrist and took my pulse. I smiled and contemplated definitions of the largest numbers in the encyclopedia. I drew a picture of the beach and computed the number of grains of sand. Driven by a private need to understand the components of things that were mundane, or frightening, or sensual, or awesome, I went through my world smiling.

Sometimes my absent-mindedness revealed itself in my school work. I left whole tests blank, smiling as I handed them in. Other times I delivered excellence. My teachers thought it might be the allure of science that made me so quiet and odd. They gave me leeway to conduct scientific experiments and submit projects that had nothing to do with the curriculum. With the help of my friend Ray, I designed a lightning generator. Dad spent hours making a Fiberglas box to house part of the electrical circuit. After we'd finished, we brought it to my school, where I gave a speech to my science class about Tesla coils. Then, with my friend Peter hovering nearby, I turned on the current. A thin, orange-white spark bolted across the table to his head. The shock caused him to bray, which caused the class to squeal in laughter. He survived without harm.

With that project I earned a merit badge for electricity, the last one I needed to make the rank of Eagle. I was two months short of thirteen. Someone told me that I was the youngest Eagle Scout on record in Florida. I had done it without cheating and without using Dad's influence to get me promoted, but I remember believing that everyone probably assumed that he'd had something to do with my success. My whole family, my grandmother, and uncle, and even my science teacher, came to the county courtroom for the awards ceremony. My minister gave a speech, quoting Longfellow:

> The day is done, and the darkness
> Falls from the wings of Night,

As a feather is wafted downward
From an eagle in his flight.

I am told that my minister challenged me to become an inspiration, to soar through storms, to achieve not for myself but for others. I do not remember this.

Our newspaper published a little story and a photograph of the event. Not long ago I looked at the picture taken in 1966. My mother and father are standing beside me. Dad looks like he was a very happy man, much more relaxed than I, broad shouldered and decent, his hand on my shoulder. Mother looks on with a perfect reflection of love and devotion. I was still a little boy, with long black bangs across my forehead, skinny arms unnaturally at my side, and a smile that asked no questions.

8

_____

1968   I BEGAN TO SPEND TIME AT OUR COUNTRY CLUB, SWIMMING
and taking tennis lessons. One spring day, Vincent showed up at the court.
I'd never seen him before. He attended a private school. When he smiled
at me, my first thought was that he'd come to save me. How he would
do it, or exactly what it was I needed to be saved from, I didn't know.
All I knew was that he was sure of himself and savagely handsome. He
surprised me. I was terrible at tennis, but he actually wanted to be my
friend. It wasn't long before I invited him to come with me down to the
beach to go exploring. We took my boat to the inland marshes, through
the tea-colored water that courses along the saw-grass islands. There, in
the intertwined creeks, we searched for ospreys, cormorants, ducks, and
snakes; we saw fiddler crabs at low tide; we sat still, watching the clouds
at sea grow into thunderstorms. When I saw how fascinated he was with
my life there, I felt magical and secure because this place that Vince liked
was me, it was my private world, the best part of me I knew.

At the mouth of a creek by Rattlesnake Point, a place far to the west
of our cabin, stood a huge scarred pine tree. One summer morning when
we were fourteen we carved our initials into one of its thick, crooked
roots. We paddled away and I looked back. This is where we'll remember
becoming best friends, I told myself. The uppermost part of the tree had
broken off in a storm and at the top balanced a great nest of sticks, the
home of an osprey. We watched it hunt. Just offshore, it hesitated over
the water, plunged toward the surface, and yanked a fish into its talons.
The bird climbed into the sky, dripping water into the sea, crying its song
of exultation.

Vince and I took the boat a mile offshore to the flats. The water became
so shallow there that low tide exposed the sea bottom, revealing seaweed
and sandy tide pools full of miniature, sometimes immature, forms of

sea life. At the ebb tide the seaweed snapped and spit as scallops tried to escape. Listening for them became a game for us. To be successful, the hunt called for absolute stillness, silence, and a quick pair of eyes. Good days brought us buckets full of scallops. Nothing was better than bringing them back to boil and dip in melted butter.

At high tide we ran fast, spotting little sharks and hunting diamond-shaped stingrays that we speared and used for shark bait. More often than not, we would stalk a large stingray, sweeping faster and faster toward the creature—only to see it glide like a phantom to places and depths we imagined no one must know about.

It became a sport that took up our summer days. I longed for those hours when only the two of us would own this vast tidal sanctuary. When no wind blew and the surface lay slippery flat, Vince rode on the bow of the boat and hung his legs over the side, flaying the water with his toes. We passed wordlessly, streaking over patches of sandy soil and seaweed, hunting for submerged landmarks. When we found a familiar spot, we were lifted into mastery of our territory, confident in ourselves as only fourteen-year-olds can be. Though our island disappeared at high tide, we knew its boundaries always. There was mystery in this water and it belonged only to us and to the elusive creatures we chased. No one, no one knew this part of the earth better than we.

Farther out was deeper water and beyond that the reef where we would put out shark lines. We hung the bait on a thick hook and chain, which led to a hundred feet of line kept afloat with empty bleach bottles. At the other end we attached a couple of cement blocks, which anchored the shark line in the water.

After catching a few small sharks, we made an attempt with a huge stingray, setting the line in a deep channel that ran along the edge of the reef. Whenever a shark took the bait, the buoyancy of the bottles and the cement anchor dragging over the bottom would wear him down, making him easy to pull in.

The next morning we set out for the reef. Rough seas slowed our pace, but after an hour we finally approached the shark line. The bottles were bobbing wildly in the waves. I yelled to Vince. Both of us watched, awed. We eased the boat alongside the line. There it was, a huge angry tiger shark as long as our boat, whipping its tail like a madman's sword. I took the line in my hands and pulled, but I weighed 135 pounds and the shark weighed half a ton. When he swam, he pulled our boat through the waves. Vince managed to throw a lasso around the tail. I tied my end of the line to a transom cleat. Now it was secure, and I sat down trembling. I realized how frightened I'd been. Vince appeared to be stunned. He had his hands on the gunwale and was peering over the side, absorbing the creature's massive and grotesque beauty. We looked at each other and wondered how we had been able to summon up such a beast. We weren't really shark catchers—we were just playing, and, well, look what happened. We laughed.

We had a four-mile trip home. With our little boat we had to run a slow engine. It was a tedious hour and we hardly spoke. Now and then we looked behind us, as if to make sure the shark was real. It was. It was too real, a dying monster. It dived below the surface and tugged so hard that I am surprised it did not rip the transom off the boat.

We arrived at shore, jumped into the shallows, and untied the lines. We pulled the shark toward the beach until it was half out of the water, and then we collapsed beside the creature, delirious and exhausted. Children and dogs noticed the shark from down the beach and they ran toward us, their parents following. A black Labrador retriever trotted up to the shark's tail, sniffing. The shark, still alive, whipped his tail and slapped the dog's nose. The dog barked and its owner laughed.

I took a knife and squatted to slit open its belly. Out fell seven horseshoe crabs. Vince lined them up on the sand, smallest to largest. Mr. and Mrs. Gavenport, an older couple who lived in a particularly well-kept cottage down the beach, walked up to us. The Gavenports had always been friendly to me, and today they spoke with wide-eyed fascination, in unison.

"Why would a shark eat a horseshoe crab?" they asked.

Vince didn't know. I didn't know. I looked at the shark's jaws as if to ask it the question. "The shark mistook the crabs for stingrays," I said, making up my answer. "Sharks love to eat stingrays. They don't know the difference." I watched the Gavenports for a reaction.

Mr. Gavenport acknowledged me with a courtly nod, as if my answer made all the sense in the world. He studied the shark's lusterless black eyes, its five gill slits, its rows and rows of sharp teeth, and then grabbed his wife by the elbow and marched away with the vigor of a man satisfied with himself.

With Vince holding the animal's head, I carefully sliced the meat above its gum line and began to cut out its huge jaws. The meat was tough, and the beast, now dead, was already stinking in the heat. Its sandpaper hide quickly dulled my blade. I scraped my skin. Rows of razor-sharp teeth threatened my fingers. A slip, and off with a thumb.

Sweat rolled into my eyes, stinging, blinding me. I wiped them and that's when I noticed Vince's golden arm pressing hard against mine. His was wet, flecked with blood. A hard muscle had formed under his skin.

Vince shuddered against my shoulder, straining to open the shark's heavy jaws. I wondered if he was touching me on purpose. I held steady, but he moved and brushed his bangs out of his hair. With my fingers inside the jaw, I thought he touched me again. Then, with one last cut, the jaws were released. I took them behind the cabin and hung them on a tree to dry.

Weeks later, after the ants had cleaned the last bits of meat from the jaws, I mounted them on a wood plaque. I affixed a brass plate engraved with the date we'd caught the shark, its length, and a weight I'd computed from a formula in a shark book: eleven hundred pounds.

Those jaws hung on my bedroom wall at home. In the year that followed, I would stare at them for hours, comforted, even delighted by their presence, as if their greeting served to defy a past intruder.

By the summer of 1968 it had been four years since Dad had last touched me. I still had no memories of it. Dad kept himself busy with his bank, which thrived, and his church, which had embarked on an expansion. His attention to me, and mine to him, diminished. When we bantered, we made tension. Usually, this arose because I did not study. He expected A's and I brought home B's and worse.

Both he and Mother adored Vincent. But from the very beginning Dad had made no questionable moves toward my friend. As I'd grown past puberty, Dad had shifted his interests away from me and my friends and toward other children, mostly the younger neighborhood boys. I know now that he managed to molest a few, but at the time that knowledge was shunted to one of the other Walts. Other thoughts kept me busy—my unrelenting desire for Vince.

I now became aware of the inevitable clash with my religion. I held intense sessions with my Bible, hoping to find an out, searching for the words from Christ that would release me from God's judgment. I found the story in which Jonathan and David sneak off to a field: "they kissed one another, and wept with one another, until David exceeded." I wasn't sure what that meant, but I had an idea. The meaning became clear in the next verse, when Jonathan says, "The Lord be between me and thee, and between my seed and thy seed forever."

The story became my fantasy but also my secret. At school I could not hide from my guilt. I took to constant embarrassment and sudden awareness of feelings at war. I loved Vince and hated myself. Sometimes I sensed that I was on the verge of going crazy. Sometimes I wondered if I had a brain tumor, pressing and growing and hurting me with its rough gray skin. I told Vince I was bothered by a serious problem, but when he asked for an explanation I couldn't tell him.

Yearning for peace, I wanted only to visit with him and a few other friends, to be private, to think, and to protect myself from being discovered. I tried to develop an impenetrable veneer, but my demeanor and inviolate smile didn't cooperate. I was considerate and very much the young Southern gentleman my parents had raised me to be. I sensed that if I tried to avoid eye contact with my schoolmates, I'd become somehow more appealing or inviting. The most effective way to be invisible, I concluded, was to look my classmates in the eye, say hi to them, and then quickly pretend that I was already looking at the next one.

My only real desire was to be with Vince. In February I asked him to spend a night with me at the coast. Because it was winter, the other cabins would be vacant, the shore desolate. We arrived, unpacked, and took a walk to the faraway reaches of the beach. At Crab Claw Marsh we stopped. Everything around me—the seas beyond the horizon, the hurrying clouds, and brittle silence—only made Vince more beautiful.

The day was ending. We heard the report of shotguns. "Hunters," I said. "I hope they don't come this way." Vince shrugged. He didn't understand how I prayed only to be with him and the hush of this intimate hour, when the sky fades to the color of gun metal and great blue herons glide toward tide pools like pterodactyls out of an ancient dusk.

We returned to the cabin. The cold night air had already penetrated the concrete block walls. We put on our sweat suits. He picked up an apple as smooth and red and meaty as his muscles. We crawled into our beds with our school books. After a while, I put mine down and stared out the window.

"Vince," I said, "it feels like an igloo in here. Are you cold?"

"Yeah."

I wanted to ask him to come sleep with me. I rehearsed the question in my mind. I watched him read. I wondered if he knew I was watching him, if he would understand how I wanted him. I felt my heart beating. I was afraid he would hear it. Vince kept reading. I watched his eyes as they moved across the pages.

"Vince," I said.

"Uh huh?"

"You're my best friend," I said, feeling stupid.

He smiled. "Yeah, you're mine too." He shrugged his Adonic shoulders, put his book down, and turned off the light.

Didn't he know how much I wanted him to come over to me? Didn't he like me the way I liked him? I imagined us sleeping together, skins making heat, my head nestled between his broad shoulder blades, sweat, fighting sleep. Say it, I thought. Say I love you.

Sometime later I awoke and realized that I had been asleep for a long time. In my window I could see bows of light shivering in the sea. Stars floated through the sky like embers. Somewhere a fire burned. I closed my eyes again, breathing my own damp breath.

The next day we went home, he oblivious and content and I in the swells of desire.

I became certain that I was homosexual. I wanted to learn everything I could about it, but I had to do it secretly, somehow. On a hunch, I drove my little red Volkswagen downtown to the state library, where I hoped no one would recognize me. Quick as I could, I checked out six books, most of them on human sexuality in general, except for *The Boys of Boise,* an account of a "ring" of homosexuals arrested in that city years earlier.

I hid the books in a nightstand next to my bed. That night, and for the next four nights, I stayed up reading, always surreptitiously and always with a school book opened next to me just in case someone came into the room. I read about "inverts" and the theories of the causes of homosexuality. I read the *Kinsey Reports.* I figured there had to be at least forty homosexuals in my high school.

Days later Mother came to my room. She stood inside the door and looked at me with an expression both merciful and disturbed. She said she wanted to talk to me. I sat on my bed, already rehearsing mentally the conversation I knew would follow.

"I found those books," she said. "Where'd you get them?" It seemed to me that her real message was Please Don't Tell Me Anything That Will Make Me Cry.

"From the state library," I said, embarrassed and angry. This is my business, I thought, not yours. What right do you have to talk to me about this?

"I want you to return them," she said. "Goodness, Walt, did anyone see you check these out? Don't you know what people will think if they saw you with these books?" Her head moved backward as she spoke, as if she were trying to retreat from her horror.

"Oh, Mom," I said in a condescending way, "no one saw me except the library clerk, and I'm sure he didn't care. Anyway, I can return them in the night drop-off box." But not until I finish reading them.

"I want you to do it tonight," she said, firmly. "You must get those books out of this house. My lord, Walt, this could ruin you if anyone found out. And it would kill your father."

I was silent. She stayed at the door. "Son," she finally asked in a changed, more gentle tone, "are you wondering if you are homosexual?"

She cupped the fingers of one hand inside the other as if she was trying to relax.

"No," I said. It's none of your business.

"It's normal to have feelings for your friends," she said. "Everyone goes through it. I had crushes on girls when I was your age, and then, before long, all that passed." She paused, then continued, treading closer to me. "Do you want to talk to Mister Sitwell about it?"

Mr. Sitwell was our minister. There was no way I could talk to him, not with homosexuals being abominations. I looked down to the thick piling of my carpet and dug the toe of my white sneaker into it. What I want, I thought, is to finish reading my books and for you to get out of my room. "No, I don't want to see him," I said.

"I think you should," she said. "And I want you to return these. Tonight." She left my room. I sped through my books, culling what I could while there was still time.

Once or twice a week Dad had been going to the hospital to see an epileptic Boy Scout who'd fallen into a campfire and suffered third degree burns to his face. Dad visited that child nearly every night for a month. When the boy realized his scars would be permanent and lost his spirits, Dad cried as much as the child had. That same night, as Mother waited at home, she rehearsed her lines, how she would tell Dad about me and my books. But when Dad came in from the hospital and she saw how upset he was, she decided to wait. He had meetings almost every night, however, and she couldn't stand it for long, so the evening he came home from a committee that was selecting the new Christmas decorations for the city, she made him sit down, and she told him about me and my books. It was, as he told me years later, a nightmare he'd fully expected and dreaded but had refused to acknowledge. My mother didn't know that, when he sank to his knees crying, she had told him something he'd feared from the beginning. As he confessed to me years later, he blamed himself for making his son a homosexual. And worse—though he never admitted this to me—I think he knew I would blame him and so would anyone else who found out. That prophecy would come true, at least in part.

He did not recover quickly. By the time summer came, his body had tired. No one could understand the hard stone that had appeared in his spirit. Everyone thought he was working too hard. Eventually, he was so weak that, on one Tuesday morning, he decided that he couldn't make it to work. That morning my mother taught her English course at the junior high school. Caroline and I sat in our summer school classes.

As I learned later, the pain in Dad's chest struck him so powerfully that he fell. On the floor of his study, he tried to think of what to do. The pain paralyzed him. He thought he might be dying. Between the spasms he gripped the rug and pulled himself to the phone. He called his doctor's office and in a strained voice told the receptionist that he was having a heart attack. Then he dropped the phone, whispered for God to save him, and lost consciousness. Dr. Linet, who'd been Dad's friend for years, was seeing a patient when a nurse ran in and told him what was happening. He excused himself, grabbed his bag, rushed out of his office, jumped into his car, and drove down the highway at a hundred miles an hour.

The doctor found Dad bent sideways on the floor, his hands gnarled into the carpet, nearly dead but taking fast, shallow breaths. The doctor kneeled over him, injected epinephrine into the heart and pushed the heel of his hands hard into Dad's chest, pumping.

An ambulance took Dad to the hospital. After a few hours in the intensive care unit, his vital signs stabilized. Even so, this was a time in medicine when little could be done for heart attack patients. The doctor knew that Dad's heart might stop in the night. He had an extra cot brought to the room, and he stayed there next to Dad through the night.

Caroline and Mother and I had come directly to the hospital from school. We waited outside Dad's room, stunned and uncomprehending. I did not want to believe that he might die. In fact, I felt so confident he would live that it perplexed me when Mother began to cry. It's only a heart attack, I thought. What's so terrible?

That night, his heart did stop again. But Linet managed to resuscitate him. Then the visitors began to arrive. In the coming days we could not keep up with them or their endless compliments and concerns. They came and they returned and they consoled us. Sitwell came and we formed a circle, holding hands while he prayed. My mother began to cry again, and I began to see that this was all very serious. People were having trouble understanding how such a virtuous and relatively young man as Dad (he was fifty-three) could have a nearly fatal heart attack. One after the other, they told me how wonderful my dad was. An elderly and yellow-toothed director from the bank came by and told me that he couldn't believe it.

"Walter de Milly is a paragon of virtue," he informed me in a wavering voice. "Only those men undisciplined in constitution—eh, smokers, you see, and drunkards—should have heart attacks at such a young age." He spoke loudly to me, as if he was hoping others in the room would hear him.

But I did not listen to the man. I was thinking. Why don't I feel sad? I did not consciously remember Mother's words when she found my book— "It would kill your father"—but someone inside me did. In fact, this other part of me had already taken credit for the heart attack. That part of me, as I now know and acknowledge, wanted him dead.

At home I sat by myself in a gray stupor, feeling insufficiently human and a great dismay to God. I roamed the landscape, wondering whether I had somehow broken away from Dad. I still did not remember the incest, but I knew, if he died, that I would be changed in some way. Just how, I did not know, only that the idea appealed to me. But so did guilt. Wherever I went, its specter hung close to me. It danced, it leered. I was evil and insane, and I knew I could do nothing about it.

9

One morning while I was at school, Mother reached into the nightstand by my bed, saw my diary, and learned exactly how I felt about Vince. Then she found my will and my goodbye notes. I'm going to run away, I wrote, or kill myself. She sat on my bed and nearly collapsed in tears.

She knew that she was going to have to call for help from our minister, Mr. Sitwell.

When they met, he told her that she should drive over to the small town of Quincy to see Dr. Harry Blount, the eminent psychologist who specialized in the problems of adolescents. It was just twenty minutes away, and she wouldn't have to worry about being seen by one of her Tallahassee friends. Besides, Blount was a fellow Presbyterian, not one of those atheistic university psychologists.

Blount saw her the next day. Concerned about my father's health, he told Mother to call Dr. Linet to ask whether he thought Dad could handle the stress of hearing that his son might be a homosexual. "It isn't too late to help him," he assured her. "It isn't as awful as you think." They scheduled an appointment for me.

Mother went to see Linet. It had been only two months since Dad's heart attack. Dismayed, Linet told her that she had no choice. She would have to tell Dad. He would stand by the phone at the appropriate hour. The next day Mother called Linet to be certain he was available, then asked Dad to join her in the living room. As they sat down, she told Dad that she'd found my journal. She told him that the books she'd found in my room months earlier had not been there because of some passing curiosity. It was now clear that Walt might possibly be on the verge of—in fact, perhaps might likely already be convinced that—he was a . . . homosexual.

Years later Dad told me that those words caused him to drop to his knees sobbing. He wanted to kill himself. I've ruined my son's life, he thought. But he was not going to tell Mother anything. This was going to be someone else's fault, perhaps the Devil's.

Later that night my mother called me into the living room.

"Walt," she said, "your father and I want to talk to you." Her voice emanated from some hideous nightmare. "Come in here."

Whatever was wrong, I didn't want to hear it. Dad sat on the couch, upright and somber, his arms resting squarely at his sides. All the lights in the room were on. I walked in.

Oh, God, I thought. They know. I felt nauseous.

"Walt," my mother said, "I found a journal in your room . . . "

"That's none of your business," I interrupted.

"You be quiet," she scolded. "Sit down, because we're going to have a talk. You have a serious problem. You need help. Your father and I are just horrified at the things you've written." She frowned. She hesitated, as if waiting for me to identify myself as someone else's child. "You're afraid that you're a homosexual, aren't you?"

"It's none of your business what I think," I said, still standing near the door. Dad's expression hadn't changed. He stared at me.

"Sit down," my mother commanded.

I went to a high-backed chair and sat down. I reached nervously to my neck and tugged at the shark-tooth necklace I'd made. I caught it with my thumb and broke it. I stared at the chain in my hand, mesmerized by the links, the sharp serrated teeth.

"Son," Dad said, coming alive, "I'd be so mortified, ashamed . . . just sickened if word got out that you were a . . . homosexual." His voice shook with emotion. "I'd rather blow my brains out than have a son who's a homosexual." The arteries in his eyes grew dark and salty. "Your mother has had to be very strong through all of this, and I want you to listen to her."

"There's a psychologist who wants to see you," she said with an attempt at bonhomie. "He's very good at helping boys with these problems. You can tell him anything. He'll keep your confidence."

I want to die, I thought. I stared at a wood plank in the floor.

"So you will see him, right?" Dad said.

I shrugged my shoulders. Dad stared again.

"What does that mean?" my mother wanted to know.

"I don't know," I said.

"You don't know? You don't know?" my mother asked, incredulous. "Don't you think you have a problem?"

"I don't know."

"I think you do have a problem," she said.

"I don't think he can help," I said.

"You don't know that," she told me.

"That's not what I mean," I said.

"Then what do you mean?"

"It's just that it doesn't matter," I said. "What I wrote doesn't matter." I felt empty.

"What you wrote," my mother said as she elegantly turned the palms of her hands to the air, "matters very much. It's a cry for help. Your letters, those suicide notes, you must be awfully unhappy. Don't you want happiness in your life?"

"Maybe," I said vapidly.

"Then give him a try."

"When does he want me to see him?"

"Sunday afternoon at two," she said.

The best thing about it, I told myself, was that, with my own psychologist, I wouldn't have to talk to my parents about my sexuality any more.

I don't think any of us slept that night, but our house was very still, the silence nourished by unspeakable fears.

This was 1969, the year of the Stonewall riots. Only fifteen years earlier the Florida legislature, sitting just four blocks from Dad's bank, had embarked on its version of McCarthyism, focused not so much on communists but homosexuals. The Florida Legislative Investigative Committee, led by state Senator Charley Johns, had gone on a hunt to ferret out—and run off—all the degenerates and sex perverts in the government, not to mention the entire citizenry. No one wanted homosexuality to "set in," not in Florida, not anywhere.

I knew nothing about Stonewall, and little about the Johns Commission, when I drove over to see Blount for my first visit. He received me immediately but cautiously, as if he was trying to conceal his abhorrence. I sat across from his desk in an office chair and pushed against the backrest. I felt sullen, even curious. I was also afraid. I tried to read the titles of a few books stacked on a metal table.

Blount put his arms on his desk. He got his message across plainly and without delay.

"Have you heard about the choirmaster at St. Mary's?"

"No."

"You didn't see the paper? It was a huge scandal. He was arrested at the bus station for performing homosexual acts in the men's room. Do you want to be humiliated like that? Can you imagine how you'd be treated?"

"I guess."

"Look," he said. "Homosexuals like that choirmaster have miserable lives. I mean, he had to leave town! It's a horrible, lonely existence. Can you imagine what it would be like to grow up and not have a nice family like yours? Do you realize how fortunate you are? I'm telling you that you're lucky because we caught you so early."

"Because I can change?"

"Right. At your age, it's not too late. You and I are going to work together to make you into a healthy, handsome heterosexual young man. That's the task at hand."

In a matter of moments I glided into oblivion. I could see and hear, but a new Walt came forward. It was as if I was hiding offstage. Usually, I stayed awake during the sessions to listen while the new Walt did all the work, but if Blount got too difficult, I'd go to sleep. That's why I remember some sessions, or part of them, but not all, not the whole of the therapy. Even if he noticed the transformation in my persona, Blount could not have understood whom he was looking at. At the time, both incest and the dissociative disorders were considered so rare as to occur in one person in a million.

The new Walt, the cool deductive politic actor, studied Blount. He was an all-around man. A stuffed bass and a rack of antlers hung on his wall, he chewed on cigars, and he had hairy arms that seemed to belong more to a farmer than a psychologist.

"What we're going to do is sublimate your homosexual tendencies," he announced confidently, as if he was planning a birthday party or a battle strategy.

"Sublimate? What does that mean?" Walt asked softly, analytically.

"Consider an onion, with its many, many layers," the doctor said. "Your personality is like this. As you work on yourself, as you grow, you'll develop new behaviors and feelings—layers of a new life which will simultaneously cloak your homosexual urges beneath a heterosexual personality and allow you to gratify yourself in socially acceptable ways."

"I think I understand," said Walt, lifting his eyebrows. This process sounded vaguely familiar.

Blount smiled. "Good. Your mother told me you're interested in medicine. Right?"

"Yes," Walt said. "I want to be a surgeon."

"Perfect," he said. "That will happen. But by the time you're a doctor, you will have become a heterosexual. Your homosexual desires will be buried deep in the layers of the onion. That's called sublimation. So, for example, when you go to examine a young man's leg, you will still obtain gratification, but you'll hardly be aware of it. That's how heterosexual men satisfy the part of themselves that's homosexual without even knowing about it."

"How long would it take to do this?" Walt wanted to know. He knew these were just words, and the words were nothing—merely something strung together for appearances. Walt was beginning to hate Blount almost as much as he feared him.

"A year. Maybe less," said the doctor, putting his hands behind his head. "You can start right away. I want you to go back and get a date with a girl. You don't have to get into her pants. Go find one, ah, a girl, from the church. Just see what it's like to spend time with her. You don't have to fall in love. You might like it."

It was a directive that Walt would hear again and again. He had no intention of following the doctor's orders. He didn't like girls, and he knew I never would. So it was no surprise that months of sessions passed with no girls to report. Walt offered only excuses. When he knew that Blount was exasperated or about to threaten some sort of horrible punishment, the boy finally asked if he could double date with Vince. Yes, said the doctor.

Meanwhile, Dad was still confined to the house as he recovered from his heart attack. In an effort to allay his boredom, he took a renewed interest in nature. He studied his field guides and spent hours in our backyard tagging all the trees with their common and scientific names.

"Do you know," he said to us one evening at dinner, "that we have forty-two species of trees in our own backyard?"

"Forty-two?" repeated my mother, holding her fork limply over the new potatoes, trying to sound enthusiastic.

"Lots of sweet gum," Dad said pertly. "And dogwood, of course. Over there, in that low spot, there's a water oak." He pointed through the window to a site that I made no effort to spot. I hallucinated with the swerving wood grains in the dinner table. Dad tried again. "Did you know that when I was a boy we had a huge sassafras tree in our front yard?" He smiled and gave us a surprised look. Though his eyes had lost much of their sparkle, they were brighter and almost pure.

"I'd forgotten about that tree," Mother said, looking at me. I didn't acknowledge her. "Did you know that, Walt?"

"Yes," I said, still looking at the table, "he's told us that a hundred times."

"It got some disease and died," Dad continued. "But if we'd bothered, I'm sure we could have put it in the record books."

"I know," I said, "you've already told us that."

Dad seemed unperturbed. I didn't care what he thought. He'd been trying to pretend for months now that nothing in our family was wrong. Mother was downcast. We finished eating. Mother put the dishes in the dishwasher, wiped off the table, and went upstairs. I knew she'd gone there to cry.

Over the next year Walt visited Blount once a week. Each time the boy sat in the psychologist's office, faking camaraderie, offering whatever minimal or made-up responses were necessary. Blount suggested that Walt's homosexual feelings were the result of a sense of inferiority about his prominent father. Walt tended to agree.

Again and again, Blount told Walt that homosexuals lived a miserable life. The boy could never be proud of himself if he became one. Certainly, he could never become part of society. On the other hand, if Walt changed, why, with his father, doors would open everywhere.

"Once you're married, you don't even have to have sex that often," the doctor said. "All you have to do is find the right girl and get married. You'd be surprised at how undemanding she might be. It's not as bad as it seems."

I continued to witness the sessions from my place behind the curtain, and I knew the feeling that being myself meant being wrong. It is clear, as I look back on this fiasco, that therapy reinforced and compounded my mental disorder, which had begun at Black Sink when I was three. Dad had used me, but the sessions with Blount made me into antimatter. I could not exist as one person. So I continued to be the everyday Walt, while the other Walt became The Patient, a kind of passive defender, a decoy boy for the psychologists.

During our final year of high school, when Walt saw Blount at least once a month, I managed, despite my quiet nature, to remain identified with the best cliques. But I felt most comfortable with some of the less popular students, especially the shy and brainy ones. Before school each morning I would stop by the side door of the school, where they hung out. We'd talk, commiserate, and joke; then I'd head to the front steps, to the "in" crowd, where the cheerleaders and the football players hung out.

Dad encouraged me to date. Mother pestered me, as did Blount, each hoping to find hope. I knew that Mother's embarrassment at having a gay son was so excruciating that she might be going crazy. I began to see signs of cracking, of nervousness, hypervigilance, fantasies. She appeared to live in a state of perpetual delusion. Maybe she told herself that her son was cured, that he was seeing Blount now only for the finer points. Her enthusiasm, when it came, seemed fragile, surreal, and apprehensive.

I wanted only to be left alone. I had nothing to share with my parents any more. If they didn't like who I was, then they wouldn't know anything about me. I managed to keep my homosexual self under wraps. As my high school graduation approached, Blount told Mother that there was hope. All I knew was that I had been rejected by the people I loved.

Dad recovered from his heart attack. He abandoned his Boy Scout camping trips and quit some of his civic duties. But this did not affect his ability to make friends with boys. One weekend he took two neighborhood children on an overnight boat trip. The next afternoon, when he returned, I was in the garage. Dad got out of the car slowly and looked at me with a sad, serious smile.

"What happened?" I asked.

"Nothing, son," he said. "We didn't catch anything." He began to take gear out of the trunk.

"By the way, your fishing rod . . ." he started to say.

"My fishing rod?" He'd given me an expensive rod a year earlier, on my sixteenth birthday.

"Robby lost it," he said. "Dropped it overboard."

"How did you let him do that?" I snapped.

"We were trolling. Robby wasn't paying attention."

"So he just dropped it?"

"It sank."

You were playing with those boys, came a voice within me. You were so hell-bent on grabbing their crotches that you just let everything go.

"You're going to get me a new one?" I asked tensely.

"Don't you get angry with me," my father retorted. "It's nothing to worry about. Next time you want to go fishing, we'll get you another one."

Don't plan on it, the voice said. We're not going to go fishing any more. We're not going to be doing anything together.

You are evil for thinking these things, came another voice. You are evil. Your father cannot help himself. Can't you see how weak he really is?

10

NATURE SELDOM IGNORES THE BROKEN PIECES OF A CHILD'S LIFE, AND during my first year of college she began fooling around with mine. I had decided to become a doctor, and I entered Oxford College of Emory University, where I could begin my path to the Emory School of Medicine. The college had only four hundred students and a freestyle academic intensity that appealed to me. I felt comfortable with the school. My father had studied there. The sense I had was that they knew my dad at the school, so they'd look out for me.

But no one could have predicted what would happen. Practically the minute I stepped on campus the fall of 1971, yet another Walt awoke inside me. There was no way, when I was seventeen, that I could know about him or the other living, separated fragments of my personality. All I knew or felt in those first months of college was the presence of a velvety pain, soft and old and obscure. It touched me too much and it made me crazy. I took to slinking to class only on certain days and at certain hours, when I didn't hurt as much or when I thought the lectures would entertain me. As my professors began to hand me back my dismal test scores, the dean called me to his office and suggested that I drop out.

When I returned to Tallahassee, Blount suggested that I get a construction job. The recommendation irked me, not least because I'd worked in the hospital emergency room over the previous summer. As an orderly I'd helped the nurses and doctors treat every trauma, from gunshot wounds to attempted suicide-by-roach-tablets. It had been a natural job for a boy on the path to doctorhood. Now, however, by languishing in a cosmos of melancholy and missing so many classes in my first months of college, I'd virtually assured my exclusion from medical school.

My psychologist thought that the construction work would serve not only to shock me out of my despondency but to make a man of me. Soon after I took the job, his first expectation was fulfilled. My boss gave me a flatbed truck to drive, but when I climbed a hill toward the busiest intersection in Tallahassee, I got confused about the gears, pulled the wrong lever, and dropped a load of cement blocks in the street. I don't know whether the woman driving the car behind me was able to conceive of an explanation for my little project, but she did manage to leave the scene unharmed.

I quit that day and told Mother I was ready to go back to school.

Chief among my early discoveries this second time around was a new friend, Wallace. He'd first appeared at school in his ancient rusting Buick, which he fondly called Anastasia. "We come from the hinterlands of Georgia," he'd announced, "sixteen years old and the dear girl is falling apart already. My Buick, that is, not myself."

I deduced that Wallace was a homosexual. Although he wasn't the kind of guy you'd imagine holding a chain saw, neither did he fit the swishy stereotype. He had a round face, like an almost-plump rose gardener, a little content and a little aunty-ish. He had a way of drawing his posture back at the top, in a delighted wobble. His blond mane dropped to his shoulders, though when he talked it flew around the air.

We engaged each other in a campaign of friendship. From the very start we took to conversations that often lasted till sunrise. Wallace discussed his interests—opera, his hair, and his crushes—while I listened— either rapt or laughing— and occasionally offered some molecule of response. Never had I met such a brilliant and flamboyant wit. Nor such a loud, giggly Southern voice. He'd play the records of his favorite divas and teach me to recognize the vocal distinctions of, as he fondly called them, Guillotine Price, Beer-Gut Nihlsson, and Monsterfat Cowbelly.

Around Wallace, my state of embarrassment gave way to silliness. When he laughed, his long hair flying, I laughed too. I forgot my genteel Southern deportment and discovered that, just like Wallace, I possessed an irreverence, a heightened awareness that the inequities in my life came mostly from the sins of my culture. He made it easy for me to tell him I was gay, even though I was not attracted to him. I was still in love with Vince, who had by now gone on to college up north. Wallace, if he was attracted to me, didn't tell me. We seemed to know that what we needed more than sex was a kind of unbewildered friendship.

But like so many others with an exuberant nature, Wallace had his dark moods. His laughter could peal from one end of the dorm to the other, yet just as quickly it could lose its easy passion, and, with little warning or visible reason, he'd descend into self-recriminations.

Early on Wallace had told me that when he was eight years old, an aunt had come to take him out of school for the day. She wouldn't say why she'd come or where they were going. But soon, when they'd gotten to his house, his aunt had explained that earlier in the morning his mother had pointed a gun to her head and killed herself.

I feared that Wallace would follow her. At a level I was hardly aware of, I felt responsible for him. He needed looking after, not in any ordinary sense but in the manner of acceptance and understanding. That I was the one to provide this was perhaps a reflection of my own needs. He seemed to have the capacity to know the truth of his childhood. In his humorous way he dealt with his fears. "There's no anoia like paranoia," he cautioned me. He told me, with ultravivid narration, of his upbringing, of the details of his mother's death, of his fears, sadness, and devastation. I couldn't offer anything comparable. I knew few unpleasant specifics, the majority of which centered around my parents' rejection of my homosexuality. Though I didn't register it—for one does not know what one does not know—I had amnesia about my own youth.

One night soon after I went to bed, I entered that confusing, hypnogogic state where images sway back and forth and the outer skin of dreams makes the first contact with the mind. I saw the smoky light of a moon slanting against the green cloth of a long forgotten but too familiar tent. I was a boy lying in a sleeping bag. My dad was with me. It was dark in the tent. It was very quiet, except for the breathing. His hand was around my penis. I was burning.

Flushed and confused, and fully awake in my dormitory room, I threw off the covers. I sat on my bed, my heart racing. The hand came back, stunning me. This was not a dream. This—this contemptuous furious explosion—had been, as I instantly realized, the first orgasm of my life. It had erupted inside the very firm and real Christian palm of my father's right hand. I wasn't even eleven. I wasn't even old enough to ejaculate. I seethed in my darkened room. God damn him. God damn him to hell. The fucking hypocrite, paying Blount to make me straight.

Now I could sense the presence of a mechanism inside me, madly working, intricately laying out strategies of vengeance. I told myself to stop it. In the months that followed I told myself that I could do nothing to my father that wouldn't hurt me as well. I can only guess why that memory returned to me when it did. For one thing, because I was away from home, Walt felt safe enough to wake up. Maybe, too, it was because Walt trusted Wallace, felt protected and loved. We had started the first true and honest communications of my life, and perhaps this signaled Walt to follow suit. Maybe I was simply ready to know. But whatever the cause, I think the incident signaled an internal process of healing.

The first repercussion of my new remembrance occurred one July morning at breakfast, not long after I'd come home from school. Mother, her expression grim, sat across from me.

"Walt," she said angrily, "your father and I are very upset at something we found."

"What?" I asked, suddenly sick.

She spoke in a stern, exasperated voice, one she hadn't used since I was a young child. "Your Dad saw a letter on your dresser last night."

"Oh." I looked down without expression, but I was furious. It was a letter I'd written to Wallace.

"Walt," she said, "you've made your father very sick. How could you do this to him?"

"Me do this to him?" I asked. "Look Mother, I can't help who I am. I'm not going to change."

"I can't believe you!" Mother said, her voice shaking. She put her hands over her eyes. "You're killing your father. You can blame yourself if your father has a heart attack today."

"No, I won't," I said, my anger building. "It isn't my fault."

"It isn't your fault?"

"IT ISN'T! It's Dad's fault. He's the one who made me the way I am. He took me on a camping trip and masturbated me. He MASTURBATED me, Mother. He made me gay."

Mother, suddenly pale, opened her mouth. "I can't believe this. I refuse to believe your father would do that." She paced around the room, her hands raised to her head. "This is a deplorable thing to say about your own father. You should be ashamed. You're making this up."

"IT'S TRUE!" I shouted. "Dad made me the way I am. It's his goddamn fault."

"Don't you ever take the name of the Lord in vain again!" she yelled. "You must have dreamt this. Your father could never do anything like that."

"If you don't believe it, then too bad," I said. "It's the truth. And I sure as hell am not going to blame myself for something he did." I headed out the door. I wished I was invisible.

The next morning I went directly to Blount's office and told him what had happened with Mother and how, weeks earlier at school, I'd remembered the camping trip.

The doctor looked thoughtfully at his desk and said, "Walt, you remember your dad doing this? Don't you think it was a dream?" He flicked a pen across the desk, as if he had better things to do than hear such nonsense.

I thought about the haziness of the memory. I wondered whether I was so mentally ill that I'd somehow made it up. I suddenly felt ashamed of myself. And my perception of Blount shifted. I felt as if I was looking at him through a veil. I felt dizzy.

"Maybe it was a nightmare," I offered. "Maybe I was really trying to escape responsibility by fabricating a story from something I dreamt a long time ago."

"It's common for homosexual boys to have fantasies about their fathers," Blount said. Then, with quiet ferocity, he told me: "Go home and tell your mother that you had fantasized this episode!"

I told myself I must be sick. When I got home, I found Mother at the dining room table nervously shuffling unopened mail in her delicate hands. I stood behind a chair and dug my fingers into it. Mother looked at me, trembling, hard edged. "Doctor Blount says I fantasized about that incident," I said, flatly. "It was some kind of childhood invention."

Mother's expression softened. "This is what I thought," she said, pulling her chair away from the table. "Your father would have been distraught to hear such a thing. He's been a wonderful father to you, and . . ."

Oh, shut up, came a voice. Another boy inside me nodded, his eyes making imaginary steps across the floor. When she finished, he went up to his room.

For the rest of the summer the other boys inside me remained awake, speaking in monotones, glaring at the world. I remained lost. I felt separated from my body. I lived in a perpetual state of embarrassment. I perceived myself as a light one could see through. My awareness was detached from my body, hovering around it like a flame on a wick. Several times a day I stopped whatever I was doing and looked into the mirror to see if I was still there. Sometimes I was surprised at how pure, almost beautiful, I appeared. Who are you? I asked. I imagined everyone asking for me in vain, as if I had disappeared.

When I returned to school, Wallace was melancholy. We shrugged our shoulders together, as if both of us knew that the magic of our last semester had vaporized. Failing to find anything to hope for, even laugh about, I receded further into myself. One day I woke up and decided that I couldn't speak. I ventured out through the campus. I could see myself from above. I carried myself to my full height of six feet but with a self-conscious gait, a little quick, or determined, and my head fixed at an unnatural angle to the field around me, as if I was being pulled along by a string attached to my neck. My eyes became weather vanes, turning away from friends as they approached. I wondered why I should have said anything before. Every act of communication in my life had been meaningless. Wallace seemed to understand this. He immediately accepted my silence. We met in his room and read, hushed and tender to the pain, as if both of us were being punished for talking out of turn.

One of my professors became deeply concerned. He gave Wallace the name of a psychiatrist who practiced at Emory Clinic in Atlanta. When Wallace passed the name to me, I scoffed under my breath. I preferred to immerse myself in my new quiet, waiting. Days passed. I disappeared into my room and played Wagner's *Ring* cycle. Out came the Rhine maidens. The unworldly music settled me. I stretched out into eternal giant-ridden landscapes. I listened through the night, waiting, waiting. Dawn came, and Siegfried's funeral pyre, the light of flames creeping into my room. I realized I was tired—and very afraid of myself.

Convinced of my insanity, I decided to drive to Atlanta to see the psychiatrist. He came into the examining room and sat on a metal stool, his hands on his knees, his white lab coat wrinkled and stretched at the buttons. He asked me questions. He seemed not to be concerned. He handed me a prescription. When I returned to school, I looked up the drugs in a reference book and found out that one was an antipsychotic. I raced to Wallace's room.

"Wallace," I asked, "do you think I'm schizophrenic?"

Wallace, who'd been drawing a schooner under sail, looked at me, startled by the return of my voice. He turned from his desk, put his pencil down, and replied in a calm, unusually serious tone. "It's possible. But I don't think so."

"The doctor wouldn't tell me anything," I offered, "but these pills are for psychotics. Am I psychotic?"

"Walt," Wallace said in the timbre of a kindly professor, "it's said that the eyes shout what lips dare not whisper. I don't think you're crazy. I think you were eloquent in your silence. It's the rest of us who are too thick-headed to comprehend."

I sat on his floor. "It's because I don't know what it is I need to say. There's something horrible about me but I don't know. . . . You always know."

"I know nothing, my dear friend," Wallace said, resting his hand on the drawing. "In fact, perhaps I should see the good doctor as well."

"Why?"

"Oh, nothing significant. It's only my temperament. Do you know what I am, Walt? Do you know what thing I am? A funeral procession surrounded by a traveling circus. Now what pills, I ask you, would he prescribe for that?"

"Antiflamboyants?" I asked. We laughed until we cried.

11

SEPTEMBER 1975   AFTER FOUR SEMESTERS AT OXFORD COLLEGE I forgot about medicine, adopted philosophy as my new major, and settled into my junior year at the main campus of Emory, in Atlanta. Wallace went on to Georgia State, though we managed to see each other. Emory brought a sea change. In my history of philosophy class I met an impossibly handsome transfer from UCLA.

Martin and I courted each other in the marbled corridors, amid the clicks and squeaks of shoes and the feathery scent of wax. We would go to the cavernous school cafeteria for lunch, sit opposite one another, arms on the table and hands just short of touching. With increasing devotion, we met for wine in the late hours of the day, took off to movies and restaurants, explored museums, attended concerts, and surfaced at parties with his friends and mine. Martin seemed innocent, untouched, and wanting.

In 1975 homosexuality did not have a visible or vocal enemy on our campus. It was a time of self-absorption and general indifference to the vagaries of private life. If the intellectual society of Emory transmitted any attitude toward homosexuality, it was one of fascination, not abhorrence. So I was able to forget, at least temporarily, the hate-infected culture back home.

Martin and I took a few weeks before we acknowledged our attraction to each other. Then, after a late dinner and a long drive through the dark blue city, one trembling moment stripped off the last fragments of restraint and we climbed into bed. The peak of pleasure, the first orgasm with a human being other than my father, disintegrated instantly into wrenching self-hatred. I lay stunned. Martin, who appeared not to notice, sighed in afterglow. Numbed, astounded, I found myself floating over us, horrified and free, overwhelmed by terror, by a voice screaming inside me.

I want to die, it cried.

Just as swiftly, my body drew me back into itself. But I craved the death-sleep and, with the excuse that I was very tired, rose from the bed and put on my clothes. Martin followed me quizzically with his big eyes, now sad, as if my departure wounded him.

As the fall of 1976 arrived, wherever I went the voice haunted me: Kill yourself now. It's all hopeless. You should die. I turned from my world and dogged a hypnotic trail through the campus. Weeks passed. My hair grew long and unkempt. It became ever more impossible to see myself as real. When I could not bring myself to study for midterms, I called my parents to tell them I was quitting again. It wasn't news. They had already sensed that my difficulties had resurfaced. Without my knowledge they had already met with the family doctor to arrange a rescue.

Once I was home, the physician called me into his office for a chat. My problem, my homosexuality, he advised me, stemmed from the fact that my parents were so virtuous, so proper and Christian. In and of itself, nothing was wrong with this. But I'd been raised in the pure light of their goodness and forced to abide nearly impossible standards. To be Walter de Milly's son, I had to grow up as a nearly perfect Southern gentleman. As a young de Milly, it would have been unthinkable for me to consider sexual relationships with girls. Such a thing was quite against my heritage and honor. My trouble, maintained the doctor, was further complicated because aggressive heterosexuality had never been a strong characteristic of the de Milly family. From way back, said the doctor, the de Millys simply weren't interested in chasing women. My father, a model of moral behavior, by his very nature could not have educated me in the ways of the world.

Well . . . the raw truth of it was that I'd been too protected. Nevertheless, the doctor saw hope, he said, great hope for me. Not only could I be fixed, I could use my curative experience to help others. A conversion could well become my life's calling! I could become a healer of homosexuals! Wouldn't that be a wonderful gift to the world?

I had a vision of me addressing a group of young men, enthusiastically witnessing to the wonder of transformation. I could see distraught families calling on me for help. I could see adoring mothers thanking me, miracles whirling about.

"Okay," I said, "what next?"

"I want you to see a friend of mine in Atlanta, a psychiatrist," the doctor said. "He's the best in his field." He gave me the psychiatrist's name and number.

"I'll set everything up," he told me. "Call him in few days."

I went to bed that night at the crest of a whole new world.

As I entered the wizard's office, I held my thumbs in my pockets like a cowboy and quickly surveyed the room: beige leather Scandinavian chairs, a thick-ribbed carpet (also beige), four cheaply framed and reproduced watercolors of the seasons. The psychiatrist jumped up from his chair to shake my hand. He reminded me of a golden retriever, an old one still full of enthusiasm. He likes me, I thought. Maybe this will be easy.

The doctor smiled broadly. "Sit down, young man. Why have you come to see me?"

"I'm gay," I said, cringing at the word. "My doctor told me you were good at, familiar with, techniques for . . . converting men to heterosexuality. He thinks . . . I think, that deep inside, I'm straight. The problem is that I grew up with very proper . . . I guess what some people might describe as genteel parents. They never allowed me to be, you know, a regular guy."

"Is that all?" the doctor asked brightly, incredulously. "Have you ever had sex with a woman?"

"No," I said as thoughtfully as I could.

"Let's see." The doctor leaped toward the door and looked out into his waiting room, almost panting with excitement.

"Damn," he said. "There aren't any women here. Son, if my secretary weren't also my wife I'd get you and her in the next room and let the two of you go at it. That's all you need to do. Screw a woman and you'll never go back to men. Women are great!" He spread his arms out, as if to extend his smile across the room.

I didn't know what to say. I didn't know if he was serious or not, and I was too embarrassed to ask. As I look back on the doctor's statement, however, I think he saw a young man full of moral apprehension, hindered by too proper an upbringing. His remarks were meant to jar me with the spontaneity of it all, the sense of ease, of play, of simple accomplishment.

Though I couldn't see myself bedding his secretary, I feigned sincerity. "That's it?" I asked. "All I have to do is screw a woman?"

"That's it," the doctor said. "And I'll tell you something else. You have no idea how easy it would be for someone like you to get a woman. Damn! I wish I was young and handsome like you again. Women are falling all over themselves trying to get your attention, and you don't even know it! Yeah, you've got a healthy, strong body, and you're a damn good-looking man. You'll have no problem nailing the right woman. You don't know what you're missing!"

He was right. He was so right that I laughed with him at the incredible simplicity of the whole thing. He offered some pleasantries about my school, and then he dismissed me. The session had taken only fifteen minutes. I asked him how much I owed him. He said there would be no charge, for our session had been a pleasure.

Not long after this, I took a woman home after a party. When she touched me, I lay there unmoved, unaroused, with not a ripple of passion. Uncomfortable and embarrassed, I told her I wasn't feeling well. I got up to leave. She looked at me the same way Martin had, except with her it didn't seem to matter as much, for I had never felt an honest desire to know her.

Nevertheless, the possibility of conversion continued to captivate me. I went to the library, studied psychology journals, and learned behavior modification techniques, such as "masturbatory conditioning," in which the hopeful convert masturbates as he looks at erotic photographs of women. He repeats the training, each time viewing the photos earlier and earlier in the arousal process. I tried it. I became easily aroused but concluded that my attraction to women's genitals wasn't absolute. What more there was to heterosexuality I didn't know, only that my desire for men existed at a much deeper level than physiological arousal. Undaunted, I tried another technique: wearing rubber bands on my wrists and snapping them whenever I had a homosexual fantasy. Over time, however, I kept forgetting to punish myself.

Every day I knew this with greater awareness: there had never been an honorable child to begin with, nor a heart capable of anything but a cold, harsh beat.

After a day of blurry, bleary classes I sat in my bedroom alone, peeking between my fingers at the wall. There hung the framed photographs I'd taken in my adolescence, winter scenes of the beach, Vincent caught grinning, peaceful sunrises softening the reef, and a gull climbing the air. God, let me die, said a voice inside me.

I reached into a closet and brought out a wood-handled hammer. In the bedroom another Walt removed the photographs from the wall, laid them carefully side by side on the floor, and knelt. Back straight, left hand on thigh, right hand tense around the hammer, he moved with the precision of a surgeon driving a pin into a bone and struck the glass. The crunch wasn't as loud as he'd expected. He squinted his eyes and smacked it again. The hammer descended desperately, viciously, again and again.

The walls petrified around him. Slivers of glass lay by the thousand about the room, pointing everywhere in the cold light, some abandoned, some piercing the pale winter beachscape, one slicing the white throat of a bird, others trapped in tide pools. Vincent's face lay obliterated, his eyes bejeweled in glass.

Walt laid the hammer on the floor, stood up, and saw himself in the mirror. "I hate you," he shouted, seething. "I hate you. Go to hell."

He wandered into the bathroom, lifted a towel from the rack, came back to the bedroom, and wrapped it around the palm of his right hand. He pinched a long shard of glass between his fingers and pressed it against his wrist. For an instant, it felt cold.

Walt shoved the glass against the twin tendons, searing the skin, drawing a mark, red and furious. He held the glass tightly, forcing it into his flesh. The skin broke into a thin line of blood. He sat motionless, his head bent down. Blood oozed from the wound. He smelled it and remembered a time in Walt's childhood when he had cut his knee. He remembered the cow's heart Walt had carved open. He sees his skin, it disappears.

When the pink of dawn hit the room, I woke up. I sat up and looked at my wound. I bent my wrist back and forth. Why did I do this? What is wrong with me?

Part Two

12

On the way home from our 1984 Thanksgiving holiday at my sister's, Mother and Dad and I were quiet as the dead. Our car might as well have been a sarcophagus. I felt embarrassment, not from the silence but because we were driving through clouds of black and yellow lovebugs, millions of them, every one in the act of copulation. Through the splattering, Mother sat snug in her seat belt, head half bowed, sleepy. In the first hour of our drive she had tried to make conversation about the grandchildren, but neither Dad nor I had cooperated. Dad had his eyes fixed ahead. He grimaced now and then, sucking air between his clenched teeth.

"What's wrong?" Mother want to know.

"My thigh hurts," he said. "It's probably the cold."

I didn't care too much about it. Dad irritated me. Between his pangs he asked me if I'd enjoyed the overnight camping trip with my brother-in-law, William. The truth is, I'd felt numb the whole time, depressed to the point of stupor. He had taken me camping but even that had not brought me into contact with life. At night under the canopy of trees in the woods by his farm, William had tried to engage me in campfire philosophy, but I could only stare back from my ice prison.

The whole holiday had been miserable for me. I missed Bo, my new lover. We were planning to visit the Virgin Islands in January, but I hadn't told my family about the trip or Bo. As far as they were concerned, my homosexual life was a secret. They didn't like the idea that I was gay, and I wasn't going to share myself with them any more than I had to.

I'd met Bo in Key West a few months before, at an old Victorian guest house. The first time I saw him he was shirtless, a tall blue-eyed blond standing under the bougainvillea and gazing into a small pool. Everything around him dissolved in the surreal tropical light. He appeared baffled, either woeful or amused, like a competitive swimmer who'd been given the wrong directions.

Hours later he joined a group of us on an afternoon sail to the reef. The moment we anchored, he abandoned the boat, diving head first into the turquoise water. I watched him, thinking how beautiful he was, floating and slipping below the surface, flying through the sea, shaking sparkles off his back. I leapt into the water too. There in the vacillations we touched, skin on skin. He moved away from me and came back submerged, grabbing me around the waist.

"You're good in the water," I said.

"I've been swimming all my life," he said in words that drifted out of the past.

He taught me how to make a surface dive. He told me, as salt water dripped down his brow, that he'd been born on the island of Cyprus. He shook his head, sending tiny suns arcing through the sky, and I fell in love. We spent the next five days together.

In the coming months Bo revealed himself as tentative and inquisitive, as if he'd once been scolded too harshly. He seemed to be involved in a deep, if incautious, process of searching for epiphany. His desire to be with me grew gingerly. Even so, I flew to Key West as often as I could. I yearned for him, for the strangely hidden nights when we would walk the island and embrace like lovers. We were engaged in a wandering, wine-drunk romance. I wanted it to last forever.

In the seven years since I'd finished college, I'd had quite a few trysts and two love affairs, both of which had ended after a year. I'd told my parents nothing about my lovers. Mother and Dad would never give up hope for the son they wanted. The last time they'd tried to "help" me, I'd just come home from college. Mother had approached me, tearfully begging me to go to a counselor. I was depressed and dark and had agreed.

I went to see Ellen Cates, a therapist at the counseling center of our church. I decided to tell her about one of my dreams as a kind of riddle. If she could solve it, I figured, then I'd keep seeing her. I remember sitting before her with my hands clasped, as in prayer. "There were two panthers coming out of the forest," I said, "and I was standing in a field with a rifle and I shot them. I felt guilty. Then I woke."

Ellen, a modest sensitive woman, sat with her legs crossed. She rested her chin on her fist. Her eyes, which tracked mine, were blue and reasonable, like the dress she wore.

"How old were you in the dream?" she asked.

"I don't know," I said, feeling suddenly vulnerable. "Very old. Older than I am now."

"And the panthers. How old were they?" She raised her eyebrows expertly, as if she already knew the answer.

"They were adolescent . . . however old a panther is when he's an adolescent, that's how old they were." I gave a hesitant shrug.

"And they were lovely, these panthers?" She smiled.

With her question I started to cry. She asked me why. I searched for an answer.

"Who were you in the dream?" she asked.

"My father?" I guessed, unsure.

"Why would your father kill two adolescent panthers?" She seemed concerned or confused. I couldn't tell which.

I didn't know what to say. I thought perhaps she knew. I realized another part of me had the answer, and that idea—that there might be another part of me—so stunned me that I lost the whole thought.

"Walt," she asked again, startling me, "what happened in your adolescence?"

I lost Vincent, I thought.

Ellen was watching me, waiting. "I guess it ended," I said. "Adolescence was the only time I was ever happy and free."

"Do you blame your father? He pulled the trigger? Or was it you?"

"Why would I do it? How could I be the hunter and the hunted?"

"Sometimes it has to be," she said. "Sometimes we have no choice, and we have to go on and leave part of our self behind. Did you love the other panther?"

"Yes," I said, crying.

"It was over, wasn't it?" she asked. "Your friend could not grow old with you, could he? He wasn't like you, was he? And it had to come to an end." There was silence. "You blame your father," she said, pausing again.

I said nothing. Then she told me that she thought we had a lot to talk about. I left the office thinking that there was more to the panthers than either Ellen or I knew.

I wanted to see her again. I had a new dream to share with her, about infant twins that had been my sons. When the day came for the session and Ellen and I had seated ourselves opposite one another, she began by telling me that she had some news. She was going to get married, and she would be moving away. This would have to be our last session.

After Ellen, I decided No More Therapists. I forgot about the panthers and the twins and who shot whom.

Wallace had become my true counselor. When my last affair crumbled, we'd talked.

"You can never see a clear image of yourself," he told me, "hence, no one can see a clear image of you. There are no measures by which anyone can place you—because you never attempt to conform to any of the games of life. You defy placement. You endeavor to find out who you are through your lovers, but you never succeed because they are but ephemeral images."

I didn't fully understand, or want to understand, Wallace's observations. As I'd grown older, I'd learned to forget most of the intrusive thoughts, the voices, the softened cry of who am I? the sense of life as a dream. It was all simply the way life was, and I had learned to tune it out. I tried to believe in positive thinking.

Dad and I were doing well these days. He had retired from the bank in 1982, and now we were running the real estate investment business together. As a consequence, it seemed that my self-image was improving. It was easy to work with Dad. Equilibrium had been established early on, for he'd quickly recognized my heretofore undiscovered talents at finance. On the other hand, I depended on him for a mature sense of business management. In the past few years, as we'd become more successful, I'd gradually come to a conception of myself as a young man with a well-earned authority.

I snapped out of my reverie, speeding along the interstate, catching shallow breaths, my eyelids heavy. There was the emptiness, the silence in the car, the backscatter of incomprehensible feelings. I looked at Dad in the rearview mirror. He was getting old. That irritated me too. The last time we'd been happy together, I was ten years old, and he'd taught me to water ski. On my first try he pulled me through the water for what seemed a mile, and I came back jubilant.

Late in the afternoon our sarcophagus pulled into our driveway. Thanksgiving was over, and I was already thinking about New Year's Eve. Bo and I would be sailing again, this time in the Virgin Islands.

At December's end we flew to Charlotte Amalie and chartered a cherry-red, thirty-eight-foot boat captained by a Finnish expatriate and his Peruvian wife. They took us to the island of St. Johns, where we anchored in the company of a few other boats. The Peruvian mate prepared dinner for us, and then we settled in for the evening. We could hear voices from the other boats, faint and happy and musical. People were popping champagne bottles and dancing on the decks. Mast lights swayed in the gentle breeze. Bo and I crawled into the cozy V-berth. We opened the overhead hatch and gazed at the stars.

Bo nudged himself against me. I put my arms around him. He wanted to have sex. I froze, paralyzed with pain.

"What's wrong?" Bo whispered.

"I don't know," I said, whispering, feeling only despair. I had my eyes locked on the stars, and I tried to look at Bo, but my eyes would not move, and I could not make myself understand why I felt such terror. I could not hear the thoughts of the other Walt, the mummified child now awake in terror because of the open hatch, the stars, another night, another boat . . . the water laps against the hull and Dad breathes on me, he moves his arm down and takes me . . . LEAVE ME ALONE.

"Come on," said Bo, gripping my shoulder. "They won't hear us." The captain and his wife were sleeping only a few feet away.

"I know," I said, lying still.

Bo moved closer and kissed me again. "Are you upset about something?"

"No," I said, going back with my eyes to the hatch, "I don't know what's wrong." I wanted to cry. I didn't understand. The stars slid around. I thought I was dizzy. It's the boat swinging on the anchor, I told myself. It hurts, said the boy.

"I can't believe this," Bo said, hauling himself away from my arms. "You're so bullheaded."

"I'm sorry," I said, confused. "I'm sorry."

I ached to touch him, but I could not move. Bo turned his back to me. I tried to sleep. I saw islands roaming across the sea.

Now I was drinking water. I spilled it on myself. Dampness. Am I sweating? I looked up. Bo woke with me. The stars were gone. It was raining through the hatch.

"Dammit," I said.

"It's all right," he said as if he was apologizing. I sat up and closed the hatch. Bo took my arm over his chest.

"I love you," I said softly.

"I know," he whispered.

I slept, dreaming down a darkened sea. Again, I awoke. The shower had passed. The hatch was open again. Starlight fainted on crumpled sheets where Bo should have been. I realized that he was awake, sitting against the far bulkhead with his arms around his knees, watching me, his gaze sad and searching.

13

I PLEADED WITH BO TO COME LIVE WITH ME, BUT HE REMAINED TENTATIVE as ever and in Key West. If my real estate investment business had not required so much of my attention, I would have moved there. My father and I worked together every weekday at the office, and we never discussed my friends, my nights, my weekends, my deepening determination to make my relationship with Bo a permanent one. My mother and I communicated even less. What closeness we'd had in childhood was gone, and, so far as I was concerned, it would remain that way as long as she insisted on believing that some day I would get married.

My inner life continued along the same path. For the most part I functioned well and maintained an aptitude for optimism. This was my mind's way of protecting me from itself. I did not have clear memory of the seizures of pain and despair. After the trip to the Virgin Islands I forgot the night in the boat with Bo. I forgot all such moments in my life. Some thoughts are like voices, and every night before I fell asleep I heard, Something is very wrong. What? I asked. No answer came.

The phone call from Kenny Ashwood's father would change that. It came just a month after Bo and I returned from the Virgin Islands. The process of conferring with Dr. Hahn and coming to the decision of castration took another two months. But Hahn finally informed Mother that he had contacted a urologist in another city who'd agreed to perform the "elective bilateral orchiectomy."

Two weeks later, on a gray morning, Mother and Dad quietly left town and headed for the Catholic hospital where Dad would check in and undergo the surgery. Mother told me that they waited and waited in Dad's room, far past the appointed time.

It was, she said, nearly noon before the doctor entered the room. A nun followed him. Both appeared uneasy. They introduced themselves.

"I understand why you have come here, Mister de Milly," the doctor said. "The procedure you have requested is rather simple and quick. I've performed it hundreds of times. But I have a problem with your case. You have no pathology, right? No cancer, no growths or tumors?"

"No," my father said.

"You want this procedure to correct a behavior problem, a sexual problem you have?"

"Yes."

"This is what I understand," the doctor said. "The problem is that this procedure conflicts with my ethical beliefs." The doctor looked at the nun, who nodded. "I have to tell you that I can't do it. I think you should reconsider. Sister Mary Robert will be happy to counsel with you about this. I asked her to come with me to talk to you."

"But," my mother said, "I thought all this had been arranged."

"I know," the doctor said. "This hospital made a mistake in admitting you. We just can't do it. I'm sorry."

Mother says that Dad returned a pleasant nod. She declined the offer to speak with the nun. It would take Hahn several more weeks to locate another out-of-town doctor who would consent to do the procedure. This time Mother and Dad drove to a small town in another state, where Dad checked into a community hospital. There, he was castrated.

Five years passed before I could even begin to make sense of this act. In that time another therapist had encouraged me to communicate with Dad. This psychologist urged me to face Dad and talk through the whole tragedy of our lives.

With some surprise I found not only that Dad remembered the experience vividly but that he wanted me to know exactly what happened. Perhaps he embellished, perhaps he invented when the truth was too plain or when I would have expected more thought, more introspection, even remorse. For whatever reasons he had in mind, Dad sat before me in the sunlit living room of his house and described his experience.

He and Mother took their freshly waxed sedan on a several-hour journey to a Southern farming community, to see Dr. Cooper. Early in the morning Dad checked in at the local hospital. He and Mother completed the requisite forms. Then he was sent on a cot into the operating room.

He remembered lying on his back, his body flat against the cold operating table. Pallid from lack of sun, his hands rested at his sides, his fingers touching the cloth at his thighs. Even though he thought it would be more dignified to have his eyes open, he shut them.

"I felt as if I'd been told to lie at attention. The impression I felt was that I was dying, except I knew I wasn't. I thought about the promises

I'd made to myself long ago. I remembered myself as a child at the beach with Mother. I built a toy sailboat. I watched it, the tide taking it, fading into the bliss. That stunned me. I didn't think the tide would take it out. A pack of boys ran to the creek, calling me to come. But I stood there by the sea oats and sand spurs, crying."

Dad's eyes were red. "Those lights over me, they were bright. I began to be a little afraid, but I told myself it no longer mattered. I talked to myself. 'It's nothing,' I said. I told myself that I had to give up. I closed my eyes. I tried to be at peace. Those surgical lights were cold. I looked around at the tiled walls and then at the masked nurse. She stood at my feet. She wore a green gown and slouched over a table laid out with silver instruments. Like this." Dad put on a growling face and hunched his back.

"I tried to talk to her. But she wouldn't do anything but nod. She made me mad. I wondered what they'd told her. Then Doctor Cooper walked in. Crisp, hale, like a marine. I thought, 'I'm no reprobate. This is a medical concern.' "

"The doctor said, 'This is going to be simple.' Then he mumbled a question to the nurse. I couldn't hear what they said. But she nodded, tight-lipped. The nurse put the heels of my feet in stirrups. She covered my knees with a green cloth. It fell down around my waist. I couldn't see. My legs were spread open. The nurse pointed a bright light right into my crotch."

Dad said that he closed his eyes again and listened to the Muzak. "Doctor Cooper walked over to my side and looked down at me. He smiled and asked me how I was doing. I said 'Copacetic.' " Dad gave me a smile of hope. "Then I nodded to the doctor, like 'Go ahead and do it.' Then the doctor said something to me I'll never forget. He said, 'You know something, Walter? There's not a man alive who hasn't done something he's ashamed of.' "

"That was nice," I said.

"I thought so too," Dad said. "I thought it was real courageous of him. Anyway, he sat on a stool behind the green drape. I couldn't see anything. I tried not to think about it. The lights burned, and I tried to think about them. I bit my teeth together. The room was dark around the edges. That nurse hovered beside the doctor and moved her eyes back and forth between the tray of instruments and my crotch. I wondered if she had forgotten something. Then the doctor told me that I would feel a little sting and some pressure."

"He stood up, threw the syringe into a red plastic box, and looked at me. He said he'd be back in a few minutes while I got numb. He and the nurse left through swinging doors. I hadn't expected that. I felt alone. And that's when I thought maybe it was best if God took me, right then. You know, I had a strange thought right after that. I wondered why I wasn't blindfolded. I tried to relax. I thought of a seesaw. I was little and I rode it, rising into the sky."

Dad swayed, saying this in a soothing voice, like he was telling me a bedtime story. He continued. "Then the doctor came back in. He said that this would be over before I knew it. I could feel something tugging. I thought of a hymn: 'Change and decay in all around I see, O Thou who changest not, abide with me.' "

Dad sang the line to me.

"Then I heard the clink of metal. The doctor tossed his gloves into a waste basket and told me it was over. I felt like the world had split apart. I felt sick. Then I thought, 'I am still who I am.' "

The nurse rolled my father into the waiting room, where Mother looked at him more like the parent of a little child than a wife betrayed. She drove him home.

A week passed before I could bring myself to visit Dad. I remember driving to the house and finding him in a heavily shaded part of the garden, eyeing a blueberry bush. It was noontime and he was waiting for lunch. Earlier in the day the yard men had been there, and the sun fell on the clipped grass beyond him. The smell reminded me of the times in my childhood when I had cut it. I remembered that I'd almost severed a finger trying to clean the lawn mower blades. Dr. Ryan Morrill had stitched the wound. Once I'd healed, he'd even let me take out the sutures myself.

I saw that the blueberry bush was barren. Dad drew the dim light about him. He stood in it like he was cooling his feet in a pond. He had an air of sensitive peace, a hint of bliss and invulnerability.

He smiled at me. "My dentist gave me three varieties of these," he said tenderly, holding a twig of the bush in his hand. He'd told me this before, but I pretended it was news.

"It hardly hurts at all," he said. He seemed relieved to have it over with. His posture was still dignified. I want my dignity too, I thought.

As winter came, Dad returned to the office, taciturn and tender, privately sentimental. It wasn't unusual to see him at his desk, thinking. I could tell he was stuck somehow, but I did not want to know why. He's like an actor playing who he wants to be, I thought. Now and then my mind's eye roamed to his crotch, and I could visualize the fleshy wrinkled sac, the scar. I felt nauseated.

Though I struggled to keep him out of my mind, I sometimes glimpsed at the man with curiosity. I wondered if he felt a need to touch himself, if he reached furtively for the missing anatomy with his fingers, if the cells in his brain had made some furious attempt to compensate for the insult, if his mind had painted an image of the testicles in a jar, if he had reflected on my injuries when he flushed a bloody gauze down the toilet, or if he did it quickly, reflexively, the way one slaps a mosquito or tells his son to go to bed.

I mused without satisfaction. I could feel nothing for Dad. I felt like a boy watching a cocoon, waiting, until he finally realizes the larva is dead by some mystery, lack of volition, perhaps overlooked by God.

At night I felt impossible. Around me in a dimly lit world hung hollowed-out souls, plumes of skin setting their sanguine eyes on me. I breathed desperately and dreamed I had been forgotten. I heard a cry of the Savior: "I will smite the shepherd, and the sheep shall be scattered."

I slept in that purgatory with my hands cupped around my testicles. I dreamed that my father was dying, and it was I who had fatally wounded him. I could go nowhere and do nothing to change things.

A few weeks later I called Hahn and told him that I was depressed. "Keep your mind on business," he said. "If you're still feeling sorry for yourself after a few months, come back to see me."

14

I DIDN'T KNOW WHAT TO DO. THE BUSINESS WAS GOING ALONG WELL enough, but we also had problems. Bankers were becoming impatient and critical because of the disappointing performance of our investments. I didn't know how to respond when they called me. Unrelenting fear—of everything and everyone—flooded my mind. I'd come to the office, close my door, and sit, unable to talk myself into answering phone calls, unable to study reports, unable to make decisions, unable to talk, unable to think.

One of my bankers screamed at me every time he called. He said he was going to sue me. I owed millions of dollars and money had dried up, and he was threatening to take every asset I owned. He had it in for me. He told me I had committed fraud. I didn't understand why he would say such a thing, but I believed him and I thought I was going to wind up in jail. My lawyer said that the banker had no grounds for his accusations, but reason did not soothe me. Wherever I went or whatever I did, I felt guilty, my senses converging into one lasting intractable state: terrified paralysis.

I pleaded with Bo to come up from Key West to spend the summer with me. He came, but despite his presence and affection, I was no happier. I began to fear he would lose interest in me. I planned an emotional resurrection, a vacation in Bermuda.

On the plane he slept and I, unrested, had the sensation of hurrying, hurrying to reach escape velocity.

Soon after we checked into our hotel, we found a small cove nearby. A hundred yards away from us a constellation of boys danced on a promontory high above water, launching themselves one by one into the surf. Forty feet below them, huge waves crashed against the cliff, flinging spray madly in all directions. A boy bolted through the sky like midnight and pierced the clouds, screaming.

With hardly a word to me, Bo clambered up the rocks. The boys gathered excitedly around him. Under the bright sun their silhouettes startled me. They were an army and Bo, the tallest, marched to the ledge. I heard the boys' voices cry in unison: "Go!" Bo leapt, his arms playing the air. He dropped feet first into the water. He disappeared under the surface, then burst through, flinging water out of his hair. He swam ashore and ran to me, wet and panting.

"Come on, it's fun!" he said with big, exhilarated eyes.

"I don't know. You do it," I said.

"Come on, Walt."

"No," I said, feeling afraid. "You go again. I'll watch."

"Oh, come on," he said, half complaining. He turned around and ran back to the cliff. Anger singed my body. We hadn't been there an hour and Bo was already running off and leaving me alone. Don't be crazy, I told myself. Let Bo play.

I told myself I should go off the cliff, but a voice gripped me. No, it said bitterly. You'll hate it. You can't do it. The cliff loomed, dark and archetypal against the sky. The boys—I couldn't see their faces—seemed happy to have Bo with them. He was so much taller next to their squirming figures. In a poetic movement a small boy reached out as if he wanted Bo to pick him up and throw him into the sea.

The voice urged me to cry. I couldn't apprehend anything except my terror that the other tourists could see my agony. Someone would see me, I was certain, and ask me what was wrong. There's nothing to be afraid of here, I told myself. I concentrated, trying to make my face relax, struggling to smile, but it felt like a wince.

Bo, having plunged once more into the sea, came over. "What's wrong?"

"I don't know," I said, paralyzed.

"You need to swim," he said with unusual affection.

"I know," I said, fighting tears. "Maybe I'm just tired."

"You'll feel better," he said. "You need to relax. We're here."

I waded into the surf, deliberately testing each inch of water until I was in up to my waist, and then I sank, held my breath, and settled on the bottom. Now I felt safe.

Fighting off a yearning to sleep, I swam under water, gliding over the bottom, kicking like a dolphin. When I came up, I told myself I should play with Bo, but the voice came back: Don't bother.

I swam back to the beach and sat hunched over on myself, drying in the sun. Bo eventually exhausted himself. When we returned to the hotel, I tried to take a nap, but the pain inside me was too intense. Later it followed me to dinner, lurking in my gut—a lonely, furious beast. When we returned to the hotel, I could not touch Bo, though I yearned to. I thought about the boys on the cliff, their confidence, their trust in Bo, their bliss in letting go.

Not long after Ashwood's call, I had told Bo about Dad. I had even told Bo about the night in the tent. I told him how I had remembered it at college and that I thought Dad had probably molested other boys. But I still didn't understand, or see, or even consider, the connections between my incest and my intervals of pain and terror.

When summer was over, Bo moved to New York so he could enroll in the acting classes he'd dreamed of. I flew up on the weekends to visit him. On my first trip I saw that he had undergone a metamorphosis. His fine blond hair had grown longer and brighter, making his complexion seem untouched and pale. He had begun to wear black clothes. He looked reluctant, or pouty, or more adolescent. I couldn't make sense of it.

Yet, whenever we were together, Bo was more tender than he'd ever been—except in his eyes, which looked endlessly for a purpose or a place to rest. Sometimes when we were walking down a city sidewalk, Bo would pause as if he was rehearsing a ballet step. He wouldn't tell me what he was doing or what he was thinking. I could understand nothing about this. I knew only that he was going somewhere new. But wherever it was, I wanted ardently to go with him. I held no greater desire than to dispense with the family business and leave Tallahassee. Forever.

In the coming weeks and months Bo and I visited the bookstores and cafes, sipping cappuccinos and watching the writers, actors, and yuppies come and go. We went to experimental performances, readings, galleries. We went to a benefit for the Gay Men's Health Crisis; it was our initiation into the era of AIDS. A man at the party had Kaposi's sarcoma. It had haunted us, a thing both fascinating and horrible. Our attention to AIDS, however, lasted only for a moment. In New York I felt content and real and alive. Life here was splendid. I could live in the city with Bo and be happy and free of my false life back home.

One weekend afternoon after a long walk in the Village, we stopped in a coffeehouse and found a table by a fireplace. The room smelled of coffee, chocolate, and cinnamon. Worn wooden planks spanned the floor. People around us sat in black Windsor chairs around tiny black tables. We ordered and watched the others for a moment. I turned to the fire and stirred my cappuccino.

"What are you thinking?" Bo asked me.

"I don't know," I said. "I guess I don't understand why I get depressed when I should be happy."

"Your problem," said Bo, as he opened a pack of molasses sugar, "is that you want something and then, as soon as you get it, you aren't satisfied."

"What do you mean?"

"Like Bermuda," Bo said, "you had really looked forward to the trip, but as soon as we went to the beach with the cliff you became depressed. Maybe it's because there's never enough. Maybe you can't realize what it is you already have." Bo paused. "Remember, after our nap at the hotel, we climbed the hill and saw the sun set over the ocean?"

"Yes." It was the first time that Bo had seemed genuinely concerned. We had watched the sun sink; it seemed to take forever, but Bo had wanted for us to be still and to say nothing, to just be in the dying glow of dusk.

"You didn't even enjoy that," he said, "and it was so beautiful."

"I know I was supposed to feel something," I said, "but I couldn't."

"You spend too much time dwelling on the inside or in the future," he said. "Sometimes you need to stop. You need to stop. That's all."

"I try," I said, pushing myself back in my chair. "I know I'm supposed to, but I can't help it."

"You're getting worse. I can't feel anything in you," he said, slowly putting his hand closer to his breast. "You're so out of it. You're not there when we have sex."

I was stunned. "I didn't know that."

"Every time," he said, "except maybe the first time, you've been like a robot. No passion, no feeling, nothing. Do you hate sex? What is it?"

I was quiet. How could this be true? I tried to remember what went on in my mind when we had sex. "Maybe it's my business," I said. "All the problems there. Sometimes it's hard to relax. Sometimes it's hard not to think about all the problems."

"That's exactly what I mean," he said. "You're always preoccupied."

Over the next four months Bo continued to drift further away from me. If he had sympathy, I didn't feel it. He continued to criticize me; he told me I was apathetic, he told me he might as well be dead. I insisted we make our relationship work, but he alluded to making new friends and demanded his latitude. Sensing I was losing him, and wondering whether the problem really was mine after all, I endured two weeks of silence. During that period my fear of losing Bo drove me to the point of insight: I concluded that not only had I been depressed but that my gloom had arisen from my childhood experiences.

Wallace, when I talked to him, told me that I ought to reconsider my relationship, or lack of it, with Bo. "While it is terribly against my usual romantic vein," he said, "I recommend that you become cooler and more calculating with Bo. One can discount one's expectations just so much. Love between mates can hardly require martyrdom of one and be deemed wholesome." He urged me to drop Bo.

I refused to think about it. Instead I made the decision to enter psychotherapy again, not with Hahn but with Nathan Observe, a gay psychologist who had to know the sting of homosexual existence in Tallahassee.

I wrote Bo to tell him what I was doing. For the first time I was going to make a great effort to save us, to fix myself, to find out exactly what was wrong with me or my ways, and I was going to do it because I loved Bo.

He wrote back. "Our relationship isn't working out," he said. "I am sorry, but it has to end." I called Wallace and read the letter to him. Wallace cried. Afterward, I got drunk.

15

NATHAN, THIN AS A NERVE, WOULD SIT STIFFLY IN HIS WINGBACK CHAIR and slowly twist a pencil between his long fingers, listening more compassionately to me, it seemed, than any other psychologist ever had. Odd accentuations in his eyes made it seem as if he was in a constant state of subdued reaction, guarding a multitude of impressions, correlating every shift of my body, every hesitation, every word to his psychodiagnostic formulas.

I told him that I wanted to get Bo back. I was walking through a fog and I wanted out.

"The fog is your way of experiencing depression," he said. "This is your problem, and I think it's been your problem for a long, long time." I slumped into the couch. I hadn't expected such a sudden and charmless diagnosis. He went on. "And before you can even begin to think about Bo again, you've got a lot of work to do. You're going to have to let him go. You're going to have to work on yourself and your relationships with your mother and father. You can't even think about lovers until you've taken care of your own family."

I was watching him more than listening. He practically sparked, he was so crisp. He swirled his hands like a magician, conjuring the land through which I'd travel. He said he would go with me, holding a light here and there as I found my way.

But I was going to love Bo whether Nathan wanted me to or not. I wasn't going to give him up for Nathan. There would be no transference.

At times in our sessions I felt like a runaway at confession. Nathan instructed me to tell him where I had been all these years and exactly what I'd been into. Eventually, he took me back in time, to the old campfires, to the nights of the Boy Scouts, to the embers flirting in their eyes, my father's voice buttering the world. The coals are skulls shrunken down, crumbling, hissing, dying. Nathan darkens the office. Walt awakens. He smells like smoke.

"What is it, Walt?" Nathan asks.

Walt's skin is burning. He floats inside me, and I give him my voice to use. He tells Nathan what Daddy is doing to him; he blacks out under the pressure of rage.

Nathan calls him back, but he does not understand that the boy has left. Walt watches from the galaxy he goes to when he is dead.

"Did you see him?" Nathan asks.

Who are you talking to? I think. Don't you understand there are others here? I see a sooty-footed boy. The light cries over him. He knows he can never be touched again, and he asks God why he let this happen, but God does not answer.

I realize that Nathan is talking to me. ". . . so when your father caused your orgasm, that's the very moment you became a homosexual."

I don't want to hear this thing. I want to know about Walt.

"The boy . . . when I was telling you what was happening, it felt like someone else," I say. "Was he like my inner child?"

"You could say that," Nathan tells me.

"Let's call him Little Walt," I say.

"Okay," he says. "We'll take good care of Little Walt. He needs our love."

"Does this mean I have multiple personality disorder?" I ask.

"No. Little Walt's a psychological metaphor, a part of your own personality."

No, I'm not, the boy tells me.

The discovery of Little Walt was at once stunning and sad. I could not shake him off; worse, I sensed there were other Walts even younger and more pitiful. Walt would speak to me whenever we were alone. In his vagabond voice he'd tell me things I'd long forgotten, taking me with him to his hiding places among the stars. I talked to him soothingly and felt him blink his boy eyes. I fell in love with him.

Nevertheless, I could do only so much inner child coddling. Nathan told me that I needed to explore the breadth and depth of rage I secretly harbored toward my father. As the weeks passed, I began the work of hating Dad, never directly, never feeling the anger I thought I ought to feel, but seeing him as someone else, the truly, deceptively, insane.

Around the office I tried to reveal nothing to Dad, but I couldn't help myself. I seethed at him. People think you're the fine white horse, says a smarter Walt inside me. But you are another kind of beast. You mauled me and left me to die on the beach. You are the Devil and I will no longer speak to you.

Dad felt my hatred. He felt it enough to have another heart attack. Mother was at home and called the ambulance. He was revived, but I believe that he did not care any more.

Nathan said it was time for me to have a talk with him. Several weeks later, on a Saturday morning in 1986, I called him to ask if he wanted to take a drive in the country. His voice warmed to the idea, clearly thankful that I was at last giving him attention. When I came to pick him up, he appeared bright and happy. So did Mother. She'd dressed him in a new sport shirt, and he walked out with me on unsteady feet, seeming proud of himself, evidently ignoring for the moment the sharp pains that had become so chronic in his right leg.

As we turned out of the driveway, I noticed his sparkling eyes.

How can I do this?

I'd come in my Mercedes convertible, top down. The car made me feel somehow conspiratorial. What were we going to do? I decided to take us on a back road to the country.

As we passed large tracts of land, Dad told me stories about their owners. "Mister Weston used to come in to the bank and open another account every time we gave away toasters for new customers," he said. "He owns a hundred thousand acres." He smiled.

Dad was trying to put us at ease, but I felt my consciousness fluttering and doubling, uncertain who to be. We hummed through the countryside for half an hour, and then I took a breath and said, "I've been seeing a therapist."

At the edge of my vision Dad looked at me, smiling. "That's good, son," he said, "I've been worried about you."

You damn well should be, I thought. "He says that I've been depressed."

"I think he's right," Dad said, relaxing against the seat.

"He says that depression is the flip side of anger."

Dad quickly raised his eyebrows, pausing in a way that startled me. "I've never thought of that."

"He says that one reason I'm depressed is that I was never able to be angry toward you when you . . . did things to me." I gulped. He didn't seem to notice.

"That makes sense."

I wondered if he really understood what I was talking about. I decided he had to. I sensed that he wasn't going to deny anything.

"There's a wall I feel—I felt—between us," I said. "It keeps us from having a good relationship."

"I know that, son. I feel the wall too."

"And that wall," I said, "is there because I'm holding back so much anger."

"Then we must tear it down," Dad said and turned dramatically toward me. He waited for me to do something. I remained in my position, eyes unwavering on the stretch of road ahead.

"Let me have it, son," he said earnestly. "Let yourself get angry and tell me whatever you need to. I want you to get better, Walt, and if this is what it takes, let's do it." He smiled, which for a moment made me feel better.

By now we were about twenty miles out in the country. I began my recitation without feeling.

"Well, you used to grab me a lot," I said. "You know what you did. All the time, you were grabbing my crotch and squeezing. You wouldn't leave me alone."

Dad listened carefully, stoically, as if the two of us were talking about someone else. We passed one farm after another. I gave the speed of the car over to cruise control. Neither of us seemed to know what to do. We went silently.

Dad finally spoke. "I'm sorry, son."

"I know," I said. Dad's eyes were wet, but mine weren't. I felt bloodless.

My mission was over. I went home knowing I'd said only words. Dad and I had hugged at the end and that had been that. I told Nathan about the drive, and he said to keep up the talks, not to expect much, and to be patient.

On our drive a week later Dad told me there were other victims.

"Were they my friends?"

"Yes," he replied in a surprised voice, as if he hardly believed it himself.

"I thought so." I closed my fingers tightly around the steering wheel.

"I always tried to do it when they were asleep." He looked like he was talking to the windshield. "I tried to do it so they would think it was an accident. When I did it to you . . ."

"I knew it was no accident," I interrupted acidly.

"I knew you didn't. You resisted me that night. It was the first time you'd really tried to struggle with me. I knew I'd done something wrong."

Dad's eyes filled with a light I could not identify. Was it an effort at sympathy, or was this his moment of self-realization, his remorse? I gave him only a glance. I concentrated on the road, momentarily downshifting, racing the engine, and passing a truck. Kill yourself. Kill both of you, a voice urged.

"Let me ask you something," Dad said. "Did you ever think of confronting me?"

"You mean when I was young?"

"Yes."

"Jesus." What do you think I was doing when I screamed NO? How crazy are you?

Dad never told me enough of the truth. He said he remembered everything, yet he could not bring himself to tell me about some of "those times," even those I was beginning to remember. I implored him. I made it clear I could not get better until I knew exactly what he'd done to me. He told me he'd already complied with me. There was nothing else. I did not believe him.

Nathan was prudent about this. He made no suggestions that there was more. Go by your instincts, he advised. Only Dad and I had access to the truth.

I asked Dad what he thought might have caused his pedophilia. Making what appeared to be an earnest effort, he seemed fixed on one event when he was twelve, which he believed was the core. He had been at the beach playing with a fifteen-year-old boy who'd taken him behind the dunes and had tried to give Dad a blow job. The older boy had masturbated while Dad had watched, and it was this, said Dad, that had made him angry and had led him to vow his revenge, which through the permutations of his psyche took its ultimate form in pedophilia.

Impossible, I thought. How could a blow job from a fifteen-year-old friend turn a boy into a pedophile who would molest his own son?

"Did you ever go through depressions?" I asked.

"No."

"Did you ever feel tormented for more than a moment or two?"

"No. Except after one incident. After that I prayed every night, for years, begging God to change me. Is that what you mean by torment?"

"I suppose."

On another drive I asked him, "When did you know you had a problem?"

Instantly, Dad looked at me as if he was in love with me. "When you came along."

And then I knew. "When I came along." Not when I was ten or eleven but "when I came along." I felt sick. If Dad was attracted to babies then, it had to mean that he desired me when I was a baby. And he had taken me. "When I came along?" My god. He had been holding back the truth. He had tasted my flesh before I could even walk. He cherished those crimes then and he cherished them now. Later, after Dad had started seeing his new psychologist, Dr. Miles, and because Dad had given her permission to talk to me about his case, she told me about his erotic fantasies over the photograph of his dead baby brother.

I wanted Dad to show me his injuries. I wanted him to beg for forgiveness, to cry in rage against his own malefactor, but his composure never disintegrated. I felt both frustrated and empty.

Despite the failure, my meandering had taken me to the end of 1986 with new feelings about myself. In a series of insights, reflections, admissions, hypnotic regressions, discoveries, grieving, denying, comparisons, catharses, depressions, flashbacks, embarrassments, breakthroughs, recollections, confrontations, and acceptances, I made a most impressive progress. I began having bouts of happiness, especially when I was alone. It was as if for the first time in my life I felt what it was like to love myself. I found myself in spates of laughter, even joyous bawling. With this transformation came new tenderness for the little boy inside me.

It was not such a happy time for Dad. Though he'd appreciated his many conversations with me, he'd seemed to develop neither an understanding about himself nor for Mother, whose discomfort was manifest, especially around Dad's developing friendship with a twelve-year-old boy named Alan.

The boy lived not far from our office and had taken to visiting Dad in the late afternoons after the staff and I were gone for the day. Dad, who was then in group therapy with Hahn, had not told him or Mother about the child, not until Alan called the house one afternoon.

When she realized that she was speaking to another of Dad's "boys," she became furious and told my father he had to give Alan up.

Caught between his attraction to the boy and his love for Mother, Dad could not understand why she was so angry or how his friendship with Alan would interfere with their marriage. Mother scolded him. He felt trapped. He asked me to help him, but I refused. "You're going to have to tell your group about this," I told him.

For Dad, group therapy under Hahn meant punishment. Dad's position was that he didn't need therapy, which he made clear to me again and again. Dad told me that he didn't belong in the same room with all those sick, un-Christian people.

"There's only one reason I'm going to these sessions," he told me.

"What's that?"

"To bring each member of the group to salvation through the Lord Jesus Christ."

I was stupefied. Nothing else was of concern or importance, nor did he seem able to understand why he had gone to therapy in the first place.

That August—1986—Caroline and the children came down from Virginia for a month's vacation at the beach. Mother and Dad would spend two weeks with them. Because I was busy with work and too uncomfortable to be around the family, I decided to visit only over a weekend.

I arrived at the cabin late on a Friday evening. Everyone was already asleep. I tiptoed to the front porch and crawled into a bunk. Fans hummed throughout the house. A light surf patted the shore. I lay awake and felt the moisture settle out of the night air.

Then I remembered. I'm sleeping on this same bunk. I must be nine years old. It is almost morning, still dark. The stars are leaving the night. Dad comes out, grabs my genitals, and whispers. "It's time to go fishing."

"Don't do that," I say.

Dad chuckles. "Hurry up."

I dress quickly, go into the kitchen, extend my arms for Dad to load me with provisions, and then I run barefoot down the dunes, careful not to spill anything. I follow behind Dad toward the boat, wading out chest deep in the chilly water, holding the supplies over my head, dazed, angry, dreamy. We board the boat and go out to sea. Later, when I have to pee, Dad pulls out his tee-tee can and watches me go. He makes me and my friends pee in this can every time. He pretends it is safer than peeing off the side. But, really, he just likes to watch.

I realize that everything my father did in my childhood, every adventure, every sunrise and game and hiking trip, all had been contrived, arranged, or adapted for the satisfaction of his perversion.

In the morning Mother and Dad came out for breakfast. I walked dreamily into the kitchen. I did not know it, but the other Walts were already up. They screamed to get away from the beach house. They clawed at my insides, outraged, angry as hell, angry at Dad, angry at me for bringing them here. I could not look at my parents. I tried, but I realized I couldn't control my expression. I pretended to be sleepy. I searched the horizon. My parents had long ago become accustomed to my irritability in the mornings, but now my mood did not change as the day passed. I turned colder, remote, icy. Mother tried to be cheerful for the children, who were running about but nevertheless looked discomforted. Even Dad, who was much better at hiding his feelings, seemed hurt. I watched as if I was behind a pane of glass and just as helpless. I felt ashamed that they were distressed.

By night, still numb, angry, and distraught, I wondered whether I should leave. Young William, who was seven, came to me in his pajamas. He wanted me to crawl into his bed with him to read a story.

I smiled, but I felt self-conscious and feared Caroline would wonder what I was doing. She'd think I was just like Dad. William begged me. He ran to his bed and lay down, calling for me to come in and read.

I walked into his bedroom, to the bunk I'd slept in as a child. William was in it, looking up, reaching his little arms out, pulling at me through the air. I stood still.

"Come over here," the child said urgently, holding a book.

I moved to the bed and sat.

"Lie next to me," he said, almost complaining.

I leaned sideways against an elbow. He handed the book to me and I began reading.

"No," William said in a surprisingly confident tone. "Lie next to me, Uncle Walt. Relax."

Am I not relaxed? I wondered. I tried to make myself more horizontal, but I was afraid and unable.

I read the story to William. He scratched at a mosquito bite, keeping his sleepy blue eyes on the book, sighing, captivated, content. When I finished, I kissed him on the forehead and turned out the light.

My sister rocked on the front porch. I went out to sit with her. It was our first summer with a castrated father. He and Mother had gone walking on the beach. Caroline and I watched for them and spoke softly so the children couldn't hear.

"Sometimes I still can't believe it," she said. "I always hated Dad. I don't see how Mother puts up with him."

"I don't know," I said. "Isn't it strange? It's still so difficult for me to be angry at him. Nathan says that's what I need, to get my anger out so I won't be depressed any more."

"I hate it that he ruined your life," she said.

"Well, it isn't exactly ruined," I said. "I'm not always depressed." Or maybe I was.

"I know," she said, "but he really hurt you. A lot more than he did me."

"He did things to you?" I couldn't believe it.

"Didn't I tell you?" she asked, voice rising.

"If you did, I don't remember." I was suddenly nervous.

"Well, he always ran around in his pajamas, without underwear, letting his dick fall out."

"Didn't Mother see it?"

ALAMEDA FREE LIBRARY

"No. He was too sly for that. But sometimes I think he wanted to get caught. One time when we were watching TV, he started playing with himself. He held up a magazine so that Mother couldn't see him from the kitchen."

It was black. I think she was shivering a little, the anger and the forgetting coming quickly. I tilted back in my chair. Dad was real after all.

We rocked silently for a while, the familiar sound of wood crunching sand on the concrete floor. No breeze blew ashore, but the air was cooling. Mosquitoes buzzed past. At the reef four miles out a single light flashed, a marker at the eastern edge. Vince and I had once caught our sharks there. Tonight the light dimmed and blurred—that meant the air was damp. The moisture would condense on the porch screen as the night cooled, seeping down to the ground in tears.

In the morning I left for Tallahassee. As I drove home, I began to realize that I had felt dreamy for the entire weekend, floating around inside myself. Now that I was far away, I was coming back, or waking up, except I was already awake.

I failed, I thought. I wondered whether my little nephew had intuited my disengagement. He had tried to find a way to love me, or had needed to, and I had failed him.

Soon after that vacation, Dad collapsed on the floor while walking into the living room to watch a football game. He lay there, too weak to move. Mother called me first. I wondered why—it was as if she was asking me whether I wanted him to live. I told her to call the ambulance.

At the hospital the doctors diagnosed not another heart attack but a bleeding ulcer. The loss of blood into his stomach had left him almost lifeless.

When I told Nathan about Mother's perplexing phone call, he suggested it was time for me to begin having talks with her, just as I had with Dad. Sure enough, I found her eager for a conversation. We decided that for our first session we'd meet for lunch at a restaurant downtown.

When I arrived, I could see she'd been waiting for me. She'd folded her soft hands on the table like a schoolgirl hiding a dandelion. She seemed earnest but fragile and unsure. She studied my face. I sat erect, as if bracing myself for stabs of guilt.

"Mother," I said, my eyes nervously moving from the table to hers, "you know I've been seeing Nathan."

"Yes," she said in a compassionate tone and seemed to relax, though her voice had an edge. "Your father told me. I hope that was okay."

"Yeah," I said, feeling embarrassed. When I was a child Mother had most often used that phrase, "your father," whenever she had needed to

ALAMEDA FREE LIBRARY

be high-minded and admonitory. I continued. "Well, anyway, I realize I've been pretty angry all along. Even angry at myself."

"Why would you be angry at yourself?" she asked, shifting in her seat.

"Because I blamed myself," I said, reciting the words more than feeling them. "For participating with Dad, for hating him, for not turning out like I was supposed to. And Nathan thinks I've also been angry at you. We really don't have a good relationship."

"I know, son," she said. "And you've had so many things on your mind, you have had to carry the weight for all of us for all these years and . . ."

"What I am getting at," I interrupted, "is that I was angry with you because you didn't protect me."

She hardly paused. "Honey, I had no idea about your father. I hadn't the slightest clue. I was so naive, I just wasn't raised to know about pedophiles—that's what your father is, isn't he? I was so stupid, I thought your father was doing wonderful things with the scouts and the church—and all those charities. Everyone loves your father so much."

"But you never saw anything unusual?" I asked. "You didn't have a clue—about all the times he put me in his lap? You didn't notice anything unusual about the way he treated my friends?"

"No," she said, twisting in her chair and speaking genuinely. "I wish I had, but I never did notice anything. Has Nathan talked about forgiveness? Isn't that what you need to do, to forgive Dad and get on with your life? I've tried to forgive him."

"In a sense, yes, I need to forgive him," I said. "But there's a difference between forgiveness and amnesia. I think there's a lot of anger toward Dad you need to express."

I watched my mother. She pushed herself back in her chair, never taking her eyes off me. "If there is, I can't feel it," she said. "He irritates me sometimes."

I changed tactics. "Mother, didn't you ever have a clue? Didn't I act strangely when I was little?"

"Oh, there was one time when you were twelve and I was worried about you. You were acting sad, and I called Doctor Saunders, who lived up the street." Mother spoke tentatively, as if she was afraid of hurting me.

"A psychiatrist?" I asked. "When I was twelve?" I realized I couldn't even remember being twelve. Considering all the other lapses in my life, this one hadn't been apparent to me, not until now.

"Yes," she said, as if giving in, "you were twelve. And your father and I went together to see him. Can you believe your father sat through that session? What on earth was he thinking? In any case, Doctor Saunders told us you were passing through some phase. He felt it wouldn't be a good idea to see you."

"Why?" I asked, incredulously.

"Because, he said, one day you'd have to answer a question on some form, maybe a college application—you know, they used to have questions asking if you've ever seen a psychologist or psychiatrist for any reason—and Doctor Saunders thought it would stigmatize you."

"Dad sat there and didn't say anything?"

"He seemed so concerned, but he was so reflective, quiet. Hardly a word. I was stupid to let your father trick us."

I didn't know what to say. Mother continued. "I still worried about you. I knew something must be wrong. I went to the library and read everything I could on child development."

"You did?" I was stunned.

"Yes," she said, "I read everything they had, but . . ."

"What was I doing?" I asked. "What had I done to make you want to send me to a psychiatrist?"

"You turned so sad, so quiet," she said. "You'd go to your room and lock yourself in there for hours. Of course, I thought a lot of that was due to your personality and intelligence; you always poured yourself into any project. I thought you might be a little introverted. But your phys ed teacher said that you wouldn't play football with the other boys. You'd go off by yourself and sulk. You did the same thing at your own birthday party—we found you crying behind the house. Your grades had gotten worse. Once you were supposed to draw an anatomical section of the eye, and you were awfully sloppy with it. I remember. You just didn't care. It was the kind of thing you usually took pride in. But with that halfhearted eye, I knew you had given up hope. I knew something was very wrong."

I tried to remember that drawing but couldn't. What I remembered now was that ever since I'd gotten the phone call from Ashwood I'd often had strong impulses to take a pen or screwdriver and put out my eyes. It would have been so easy and quick, just a jab, a few inches, piercing the cornea. Fluid would drain down my cheek. I would feel pain, disgust, fear, shock, loathing. I had mentioned these impulses to Nathan, but he hadn't seemed to make much of them. Only years later did I remember the myth of Oedipus, who blinded himself when he learned that he had killed his father and committed incest with his mother.

"You continued to have problems," my mother said. "In high school—oh, those years must have been awful for you! You were making up wills and leaving goodbye notes around the house."

"Goodbye notes? Wills? I don't remember that."

"You left notes for Vincent and some of your other friends and a note to your grandmother telling her you'd gone away and didn't know when you'd ever be back. Of course, that was when I called Doctor Blount."

I realized I was suddenly tired. I didn't want to get into Blount and those embarrassing high school years. Mother and I were through eating, and I suggested we leave. I could tell that Mother was drained. We both said we'd talk again next week.

I went home, pulled off my shoes, and collapsed face down on the bed. There was a difference between passive and active lies. What kind of perverted love did Dad have for me? I thought about those early days of adolescence and imagined Mother, worried and determined. I could see her figure at the sunlit kitchen table, reading her books while Caroline and I were at school. She would be reading furiously, as if running alone through an unknown land, searching for a lost child.

16

1990   UNSHAVEN, AND HONED THIN BY WEEKS OF FEAR, I SAT AT MY
dining table shoving piles of papers aside to make room for a nautical
chart. I snarled at a stack of unread magazines and threw them across
the room. Stop it, I told myself. There's no need to panic. Serious work
lay ahead of me and it required my full attention. I took a breath and
unrolled the chart.

I was about to plot a course that would take me from Carrabelle,
where I kept my boat, down the Gulf coast of Florida on a 450-mile
journey to Key West.

Despite enormous pressures to attend to business emergencies, I could
focus only on this one mission: to escape from Tallahassee for good.
Nothing else mattered. All about my house the details of a false life were
coming to an end. Dozens and dozens of half-opened cardboard file boxes
lay around the room. Weeks earlier I'd unplugged my phone and shuttered
the windows. The house smelled like an attic. My plants shriveled in dark
corners. The putrescent slime of rotten food dribbled into the bowels of
my refrigerator.

I'd just completed my fourth year with Nathan. Not long after I'd
started seeing him, he'd invited me to a party with a group of friends
he called "The Family." It was a group he'd assembled over the years,
some friends, some patients. They'd prepared an elaborate, almost gaudy
dinner, which I suffered through, smiling, being polite, trying to appear interested. At the next session Nathan had asked me if I'd enjoyed myself—
as in, "Wasn't it fun?"

"Yes," I lied.

"Well, I think it would be good for you, socially, to become part of
the group. They are all wonderful people, and they like you."

"Won't this interfere with therapy?" I asked. "I may feel awkward."

"You'll get used to it," he said. "I've given this a lot of thought. I think you're far enough along to handle it."

A cascade of invitations ensued. I'd been recruited into The Family. It was essentially directed by Nathan. Nearly every weekend there were parties, beach trips, and birthdays. The members pretended that we were not participating in something between group therapy and special education for the emotionally immature.

But soon The Family's events began to conflict with the rituals I'd established a decade before with my longtime Tallahassee friends Lewis and Manny, lovers of twenty-five years who had taken me under their wing. Their house was a gay oasis in a neighborhood of WASPs, the only house in Tallahassee I felt comfortable enough to visit any time I wanted. They were my big brothers, strong and wise and giving.

But there was no escaping one's duty to The Family, for Nathan ruled it and made his position clear. It wasn't uncommon for him to tell me after our therapy session, "Don't make plans for the seventeenth. We're having a dinner at Greg's. You can bring the wine. Then, on the twenty-fifth, we're all going to drive up to Thomasville . . ."

If I, or anyone else in The Family, failed to attend a function, the consequence was likely to be a reproachful lecture from Nathan and a generous measure of guilt. Lewis and Manny questioned this practice, but I defended Nathan. "He knows what he's doing," I said. I believed it for years; if I was uncomfortable around The Family, it was my fault, my deficiency, my failure to develop psychologically.

I manifested two identities in the presence of The Family: the despairing inner self and the giddy outer persona filled with fake enthusiasms and patriotic devotion. The strain of being someone else, of once again giving up my own existence in the hope of "healing," became so unbearable that I had to quit at any cost.

After four years, love, purpose, and identity were still wild boys to me; I could not find them in Nathan's office or in The Family or even in Tallahassee.

I had other problems. The financial performance of my real estate investments was abysmal and had been declining for some time. To make it worse, I hadn't told my investors the truth; I had limped along, hoping for a white knight, or a turnaround, or a brilliant idea. A host of accusers came forward. They did not want to believe that their investments had gone bad on their own. They believed I had created an intricate scheme to defraud them, conning everyone along the way, including my father.

They became convinced I'd bought a yacht and spirited their funds off to foreign banks. I was the black sheep, and a few of them wanted to butcher me.

I felt the ugliest kind of guilt. My banker had pressed on with his lawsuit, hiring a forensic accountant who searched for evidence of theft, perhaps a Swiss banker's fingerprint on some document.

Ever since I'd had to deal with Dad's pedophilia, all my accomplishments had seemed hollow, and the whole endeavor of making money had become despicable. Wallace tried to give balance to my predicament by reminding me that my investors had entrusted me with their money for only one reason: "Beneath their nice Southern politeness lies the universal sin."

"And what is that?" I asked.

"Greed."

While I appreciated my friend's wisdom, I couldn't ascribe any responsibility to the investors. I viewed them as utterly innocent and me as utterly evil. I gave no weight to the facts, nor could I see them.

Over the last few years the pain in Dad's right leg had crept through his flesh like a slow-burning fire. His leg swelled as if it bore the weight of his evil. The skin turned cold, translucent splotches of yellowish white mottled the flesh down to his ankles, and his foot turned a cadaverous blue. His nerves constantly reported their own annihilation. Ultimately, Dad was so tortured that he could no longer walk. The doctors knew that his arteries were clogged. They failed to clear the vessels with potent drugs and angioplasty. With no other possibilities at hand, and the threat of gangrene imminent, they had taken the saw to his right leg. Now it ended in a stump, just below his knee.

During the night after the amputation, a blood clot broke loose from the stump and traveled to his brain. He awoke in the morning to find that he couldn't speak the words he was thinking. Sentences came garbling out of his mouth.

When I arrived at the hospital, I found the surgeon in Dad's room squeezing a mass of bloody fluid out of the stump. Half-covered in crumpled white sheets, his silver hair a mess, Dad sat on the bed cheerfully using a combination of hand signals and drunken utterances, trying to carry on a lighthearted conversation with the doctor. The surgeon seemed relieved at his patient's determination and resiliency, but I stood there in horror. The anger I'd felt toward Dad at the beginning of therapy had seemed to dissipate. We enjoyed a new kind of sensitivity. Now he was like me, a man hiding his despair and creating a reality unattached to his soul.

Dad maintained his enthusiasms throughout his long recovery at the physical rehabilitation center. The day of his release, the staff there gave him a party. From his wheelchair he spoke, carefully enunciating each syllable, just as he'd been trained, offering appreciation and encouragement to the room full of nurses, physical therapists, and patients. He cried at the end. His cheeks blushed plainly. As I rolled him toward the door, he sent a thumbs-up signal to the others. He left with hugs and cheers and goodbye kisses.

In the days before I had closed my office for good, my secretary became so upset with my perplexing behavior that she called my father and suggested to him that I ought to see a psychiatrist. Dad knew about Nathan and covered for me, but he nevertheless saw that whatever the remaining problems were, Nathan hadn't been able to fix them. Dad told me how worried he was. He told me he wanted me to do anything, anything I needed in order to be happy, and if that meant my moving away to begin another life, then that's what he'd support.

I prayed for help but no longer to the anthropomorphic god of my childhood. Whatever I prayed to existed in other dimensions, in transrational fields of quantum energy.

I had a new boyfriend. John was a perfect mathematician, a lavishly talented composer, and a bassoonist. At eleven he'd been the world's hula-hoop champion.

One day he came home to find me in the bedroom curled up in pain. He sat next to me.

"What's wrong?"

"I don't know," I said. "Everything. I just feel awful. I want to live on the sea."

Without a pause, he straightened his back and deepened his voice: "You are Moby Dick and I am Starbuck."

Then, grabbing an imaginary thing in his hands, he said, "This harpoon is your banker." He pulled it out of my body and threw it down.

"This harpoon is your depression." He pulled it out of my body and threw it down.

"This harpoon is Nathan." He pulled it out of my body and threw it down.

"This harpoon is your father." He pulled it out of my body and threw it down.

He gave me a kiss, turned out the bedroom light, and went into his room to practice.

A month before I left for Key West, he prepared for my departure by moving out of the house, which I planned to rent out.

Nathan called me and said that he was having a going-away party for me. I said I didn't want it. He told me that it was important to The Family. So I went. They had a barbecue. Everyone seemed excited and yet no one seemed to understand. The other Walts woke up, terrified. They hated the attention.

On the day of embarkation John joined my first mate and me on our drive to the marina at Carrabelle. Mother and Dad came in their car, and Wallace arrived from his new home in nearby Apalachicola.

I'd already provisioned the boat. We had all that we needed: clothes, tools, oil cans, fishing rods, charts, tackle, first aid equipment, radios, a depth sounder, Loran, food, ice, and water.

It was time to go. I hugged my excited and worried mother. Dad, standing on his new prosthesis, braced himself against the open door of the car and stood upright in his dignified and unassuming way. I hugged him. He held onto me. His eyes were red. He looked shaken. He didn't want to lose me.

I boarded my boat, started the engines, and untied the mooring lines. Slowly, we moved out of the slip into the river, picking up speed on toward the Gulf. A strong southerly wind lifted six-foot seas. I held tightly to the wheel, keeping a rigid course. I realized how tense I'd been. As the seas became heavier, I sighed. After an hour we couldn't see land.

Our boat was so heavy it gored the waves. The engines chewed the water. I turned and watched our wake. Two serpentine ghosts uncoiled from the propellers. I watched them snake behind us until they melted into the sea. They were beautiful and sad.

Three days later we arrived in Key West. Life did not come easily. I had the same nightmare again and again: The phone rings. On the line is one of my largest stockholders, a friend of my father's. The man asks in a cordial tone how I'm doing. Suddenly, his voice leaps in utter rage. He screams how disappointed he is in me. "You're no good," he shouts. Sometimes the man lowers his voice to mollify me. But then he says acidly, "You're Killing Your Own Father." Sometimes the man on the phone asks for his money back. "Where is it, Walt? Switzerland? Panama?"

Every morning I awoke and looked around my apartment, not knowing where I was. I tried to shake off the fugue by going to sea. Sometimes with friends, sometimes alone, I took the boat seven and eight miles into the Atlantic, to the deep-water grounds of yellow tuna and wahoo.

One day I decided to keep going. At twenty miles out I noticed a change in the water ahead. A quarter of a mile away, just like I'd read, I could see a river in the ocean, the Gulf Stream. It shuddered and gleamed. I watched it, ink blue and muscled, moving fast. I wasn't sure if I wanted to go closer. It would have been no challenge for me, but I didn't want to touch it, for fear that all would be ruined.

Wherever I went or whatever I did, my body felt like someone else's. Being in Key West felt strange, not so much because I'd run away from Tallahassee but because I'd run away without knowing what it was I was supposed to be running to. But an inner voice made one thing clear to me: I was not here to have fun. I was here for punishment.

In the meantime, Nathan called and told me it was time for me to return to Tallahassee. "You've been a part of the community here," he said in a reproving tone. "You were here in the good times, and now the bad times are here, and everyone feels like you've abandoned them."

"But I'm going through a lot," I said.

"Walter," said Nathan, "your parents are old and frightened. They're worried. They need you. It's been two months since you left here. It's time to quit neglecting your parents and your family."

I was too enraged and too intimidated to respond. What did he mean by "good times"? Didn't he know that he was one reason I had left Tallahassee?

A few days after his call, I related the whole story to a psychiatrist friend. "He's trying to make you into the dutiful son," the doctor said. "Tell him to go to hell."

17

1991   KEY WEST'S WHITE STREET PIER STRETCHES SOUTHWARD INTO
the shallow waters of the Atlantic, giving the impression of a roadway
once destined for the forbidden island of Cuba. Tranquil and barren, it
attracts maybe two or tree fishermen at a time and even fewer tourists.

I rode my bike there often. Today, in the noon sun, I had driven to the
end and stopped. Sweat streamed down my wrists onto wet handlebars.
I fixed my eyes on the horizon. The breath of the world came to a
pant, ruffling little waves here and there. Flecks of silver scattered across
the sea.

I watched the water around me. The natural flow of the tidal currents
found an unnatural barrier here. The pier was built as a solid concrete
bulwark running a quarter mile into the Atlantic. As a result, the water to
the east of me was blocked, often stagnant, tepid with the decomposition
of foul-smelling seaweed.

I thought of the Cubans just over the horizon. I felt ashamed that I
was spending so much time preoccupied with my mental health. Whole
cultures anguished, famine was decimating African nations, and right here
my own brothers were slowly dying of AIDS. I knew dozens of them. Each
month more arrived from whatever hell they'd come from. What moral
right had I to dwell on myself?

Not long after I'd moved to Key West, I'd met a gay minister named
Steve Torrence. Part rascal, part sage, he'd virtually created the local
Metropolitan Community Church. We talked often. One day he suggested
that I could help others who had been abused as children. Perhaps, he said,
this was the very element I was missing in my life. So I offered to develop
a support group for the church.

But I lost interest or, rather, could not connect with my interest. I
returned to Steve week after week in a state of gloom.

One day he sat back in his chair and asked, "Walt, do you think that you have honestly dealt with your anger toward your father?"

"Yes," I said, "I'm certain that I've forgiven him. I know I have."

"I don't think so," he said.

I began to believe that Steve was right. But how could I release it? A "supervised tantrum," at least with Steve, would be too embarrassing.

So I found Luke. He was a beautiful long-maned therapist of the New Age. From his old bougainvillea-shrouded house near the cemetery in the middle of the island, he offered his guidance, a repertoire of inner child techniques, a full range of movements and meditations.

With his wild blue eyes he instructed me in the art of venting. One day he gave me a pillow. "Pretend it's your father. Tell him how you feel. If you have to, beat him up."

I knelt on his floor and descended into a half hour of rage. I beat the pillow until my hands were swollen. I ripped it open, spilling foam rubber all over the room. I looked up at Luke to say I was sorry.

"I've got plenty of pillows," he said, tossing another on the floor. "Keep going."

Afterward, Luke told me that the police had come. I'd screamed so horrifically that a neighbor had called them. I hadn't noticed.

Sometimes Luke sat across from me and gently woke my inner child. We had tender conversations with the boy. As he had in my sessions with Nathan, the boy seemed real to me.

"Does this mean I have multiple personality disorder?" I asked.

"We all have multiple personalities," he said.

The summer with Luke became fresh and clear. We sat in his garden for hours. His glowing face guided me back to the horrible scenes of my childhood. "Re-create them, Walt. Give the stories new, happy endings." I had no trouble sprinkling magic through the woods.

One unhurried afternoon Luke held a mirror to me so that I could see my personas: The analyst. The businessman. The diplomat. The terrified boy.

I'd suspected those. But in a violent and beautiful insight I saw the person behind these masks: The Victim. It was my core identity. The victim explained everything. I'd entered every event in my life unconsciously expecting to be victimized, by enemies, superiors, and saviors. Usually, perhaps even invariably, I had had a hand in my fate by attracting the wrong kinds of people into my life or by making myself vulnerable or even guilty. From Dad to Blount to my bankers to the Bible-thumping masses and even Nathan—all had victimized me.

This revelation liberated me to the point of tears. I knew I'd found the answer. "I've solved the puzzle!" I said. "The victim identity has made me miserable all of my life."

The clear thing to do now was leave the victim behind. I wrote to my parents with the wonderful news.

Two weeks later Mother called to say that Dad had gone back to the hospital. According to the doctors, a blood vessel in his brain had burst. I arrived in Tallahassee still glowing from my work with Luke. Amused and suspended from all worldly concerns, I walked through the hospital as I imagined a spirit would, floating like a dandelion seed through the corridors.

Wearing the chinos, loafers, and oxford shirt I'd left in Tallahassee when I moved to Key West, I walked into Dad's intensive care unit and grabbed the steel bed rail. An electric fan blew cold air over his body. He was pale, flattened into the sheets, and, except for a towel over his groin, naked. The sight repulsed me. I reminded myself that the man was dying. He wants to be loved, I told myself.

Earlier, Dr. Alice Beyerly had come to visit him.

He was still somewhat conscious. "Oh," he said to her. "I've just returned from a lovely trip up the Amazon."

Those were perhaps his last words. He could still smile placidly at his visitors and nod, following them with his eyes. Sometimes all he could do was groan, and this was when I was certain that he was dismayed. The hemorrhage progressed throughout the right side of his brain, rendering the left side of his body useless. He quit opening his eyes.

Now, I held his right hand as if I were shaking it. "Give me one squeeze for yes," I said, "two for no. Do you understand me?" Dad squeezed once. I wanted to say "I love you," but I couldn't bring myself to do it. After a few minutes I let go of his hand and left.

Dad developed pneumonia, "the old man's best friend," the doctor said. Mother and I came to his bed again. Dad, deeply unconscious, struggled to inhale, drawing his abdomen down into his gut. The heart monitor at his side registered sixty beats a minute. Today I couldn't squeeze his right hand any more because it was heavily bandaged into a mitt and tied to the bed railing. It was how the nurses protected Dad from digging at the pain in the stump below his knee. I placed the palm of my hand on his forehead and then I moved aside. Mother touched her lips to her husband's.

Earlier in the day the doctor had discontinued all medications but morphine. Dad took deeper, almost desperate breaths, and I wondered whether he knew he was suffering and about to die.

Mother and I talked.

"I think we should tell him it's okay to die," I said.

"Yes," she said. "Go ahead and tell him."

"Mother and I will be okay," I said softly and confidently to Dad. "If you want to die, it's all right with us." I spoke with as much compassion as I could muster.

"Did you hear what Walt said?" Mother asked in a soothing voice, leaning over toward his ear. She held his hand. "We'll be okay," she said. "If you want to go to heaven now, it's all right."

Dad's heart rate dropped to fifty-five. She found a Bible and opened it to Paul's Epistle to the Romans. I looked at the large flashing numbers on the heart monitor. Forty-nine, it blinked. Forty-five. I felt myself departing into a mist. "For I am persuaded," read Mother in the voice she'd used when I was a little boy, "that neither death, nor life, nor angels . . ."

His heartbeat dropped to thirty.

"nor principalities, nor powers, nor things present, nor things to come"

Twenty-two.

"nor height, nor depth"

Fifteen.

"nor any other creature"

Twelve.

"shall be able to separate us from the love of God"

Nine.

"which is in Christ Jesus, our Lord."

Zero.

An alarm began to beep at the nurses' station.

"It's over," I told Mother. I hugged her, sobbed a few seconds, and stopped myself. I realized I was floating in the air. Mother looked up from her Bible, as if she didn't understand what was wrong, or as if Dad needed comforting. "It's over," I repeated. She cast her eyes down at her husband and saw that he was dead.

A nurse in white appeared in the room. She glided in and stroked Dad's hand. I couldn't understand why a dead man would need a nurse, but I saw that she had feelings for Dad and I wondered if he had spoken kindly to her before he lost consciousness. She reached up to the heart monitor and asked if she could turn it off. I nodded. When it went blank, my heart raced.

Dad's head was pushed back in the pillow, his silver hair soft and untroubled. His mouth was opened unnaturally, as if he was hesitating, caught on the downstroke of a confession.

Mother and I began to leave the room. Suddenly a breath started to rasp from his lungs; it seemed to last forever. It might have sounded comforting to anyone else, but the noise touched my skin, provoking me like one last unwanted caress. "It's just air escaping from his lungs," I explained to Mother when she turned, startled, to look at her husband for the last time. She looked into my eyes again as if asking me what to do. We left the hospital. Mother went home, and I returned to Lewis and Manny's house, where I was staying. When Lewis opened the door for me, I sobbed into his arms.

My sister flew in from Virginia the next day. In the hours before the funeral, she and Mother and I talked privately, sharing our perplexity over Dad's two sides, absorbing the huge infusion of compassion from the community, consoling the weeping friends who came to console us, bearing in another part of our minds the unsharable truth.

What I remember fondly about this time, however, was Wallace's participation in the procession. He'd driven in from Apalachicola dressed in suit and tie, his Einsteinian hair bursting with galactic energies. He did not want to meet us at the church with the other mourners, as was tradition. He came to our home and said he'd follow us to the service. So the three vehicles departed from the house: the hearse carrying Dad, the shiny black limousine carrying our family, and Fafner, Wallace's 1963 Ford Falcon. It had long ago become a shell of a car, chalky, battered hard, and rusted through. Wallace has never been steady at the wheel, and so I watched with amusement as our limo driver stared him down through her rearview mirror; I know she was mortified. Wallace drifted to the center line, jerked back into place with both hands on the wheel, slowed as if he wasn't sure just how close to follow, then sped up to catch us, his face alive with love and felicity.

He had seen my father several times in the years before he died. Wallace managed to keep an ongoing exchange with Dad, a kind of grandmotherly detachment that allowed them to make conversation while pretending neither knew anything.

In the years before his death, Dad had handled his own friends with a mixture of optimism and humility. He defused the potential embarrassment of forgotten names or stories by saying, "I had a stroke a few years ago, and I can't be sure if it's affected my recollection." Dad's genteel countenance disarmed those who sought to peek at his artificial leg. One soon forgot he was even in a wheelchair. At seventy-six Dad remained a handsome man, his charisma more sublime than ever. His voice was reassuring even though the stroke moved him to accent the wrong syllables and prolong his vowels. He wanted to make everyone around him feel happy.

He wanted to be held, he wanted to touch my mother and my sister and me, and he wanted his gentleness to find ours. When the physical therapist had told him he had to use a walker, he was disappointed. He'd already set his mind on a nice cane. Now, when he walked on his prosthesis, I saw him looking around and smiling, an unblemished child who wanted us to see his accomplishment.

Dad's skin was always smooth, even toward the end. His eyes, blue and intelligent and set above blushing cheekbones, still sparkled when he laughed, exuding sincerity and even wisdom.

I had looked into his eyes and tried to see a pedophile, a manipulator, a man so determined to have what he wanted that he would lure a son into existence. But I could find in him no telling aberrations, and I was the one person on this earth who should know.

Toward the end he confessed that the devils inside him hadn't died. He'd tried to numb himself, to wage war against the seductions, to forget his sin, even to chop it off.

When I looked at Dad, I feared that my own condition would deteriorate into pedophilia. I feared that my own blood would attack me, dissolving the little arteries in my feet. I feared that the same corrupted seed waited in my brain, dormant save for a signal from some patient gene.

I knew that on occasion Dad had wanted to kill himself. I'd learned this on our drives in the country. The first time he'd nearly done it, we were staying at the beach. Caroline was furious at Dad because he had exposed himself to her friend. That day he went out in the boat alone, far from land. He jumped into the water and swam away, hoping he would become exhausted and drown. People would have believed it was an accident. After all, men have fallen out of their boats since the beginning of time.

He'd considered suicide at other times too. He admitted to me that he had willed himself to have his last heart attack. Several times in his life, while on the highway, he'd thought of deliberately driving his car into the concrete stanchion of an overpass.

During his last year, 1991, Dad had written to me about his spiritual trepidations. He dreaded the River of the Dead, fearing it would be the final journey for him, the "Way among the Lost People." He was certain that his soul was caught in a struggle between God and the Devil. He feared that the Devil was winning, that a boat was waiting for him at the river's edge, a ferry to Hell.

He had wanted to explore the Amazon. I had watched him share this dream with his friends, the doctors and insurance salesmen and retired professors; like little boys they listened to the faint call of his soul. "The river is beautiful. Be still."

Dad in his last days had no doubt vanquished all the rivers, with their filmy surfaces, their simmering fury, the rivers that moved on with the difficult imperative of taking things away. Maybe Dad wanted to go so far away in his travels that the accumulated mass of guilt and obligation and knowledge would fade into deliverance, even drowning.

Rivers held a spell over me too, maybe even more than they had over Dad. Perhaps they were where I could find the truth of my father, something I wanted more than life itself—the allure and reality were always passing by, the dangers distorted, disappearing into the depths and eddies, mixed up and unspooled and lost. The passage was always murky, the ever-narrowing tributaries and rivulets closing in, the forest canopy zipping up over us until the sky flickered out, leaving us immured with the shadows and the buzz of paper wasps.

Along the way we passed snakes that leered at all prospects and luckless insects trapped in the whirling currents. The bugs spun, drunk in their fate, racing down a vortex of black water. There were buzzards, cormorants swimming underwater, turtles sunning on fallen trees, lily pads, pink snail eggs glued to the reeds. The air smelled like it had just rained. We were hot and the water was cold and our sweat stung our eyes, but we kept going deeper because we were already seduced. At night, when we'd try to sleep, we heard the incessant strain of mosquitoes. Farther out into the wilderness, where we imagined no human had ever been, we heard the murmur of drums.

A child wants to trust his father. He wants to believe that tonight the beast won't come out of the wilderness. Together they drift with the currents; they snuggle. The father laughs at the demons that watch from the bank.

What was at the source of the river? We didn't know, not when we were together. But I believe that, in his final years, my father sought the place where this world ceases to exist. I imagine my father at this mystical boundary, where he stands alone, looking back upon himself. It is here, at the source of the river, that he accomplishes what is impossible while on this earth: he repudiates his life. It is a moment of transfiguration—he finds atonement for the sins he never understood and, in so doing, he loses consciousness forever, ravished by the supernal waters.

18

I RETURNED TO KEY WEST IN A POSTFUNEREAL WHISPER. I HAD TO SEE Steve.

For a few minutes we talked about the funeral and how my life would change now that Dad was dead. I looked down at the floor. When I looked up, I was someone else.

Steve sat up in his chair, stunned. "What's happening to you, Walt?"

"I don't know," the boy said.

"Everything about you has changed," he said. "Just like that!" He snapped his fingers. "Your whole body, the way you're sitting, your posture, the look in your eyes, your voice."

I'm scared. The boy wanted to cry.

"I'm not going to hurt you," he said, making himself calm.

"I know," the boy said.

"Do you want to leave?" he asked.

"I think so," the boy said. "Maybe take a nap."

"Yes," he said. "Go home and take a nap, but call me if you need me, okay?"

The boy went home and took a nap. Half an hour later I woke up. I saw Steve several days later at an annual awards presentation given by our local AIDS charity. The next week, when I went to see Steve in his office, he asked me if I had been attracted to the man who sat next to me.

"No one sat next to me," I said.

"Yes, Walt," Steve told me. "There was a nice-looking man sitting next to you."

"I don't remember anyone."

"You were flirting with him."

"No, I wasn't."

"Walt," Steve said, "you spent half your time talking to the guy. I saw you, and you were flirting with him. Please don't think I disapprove, I'm just asking if you liked him."

"Are you sure? I don't even remember anyone," I said.

"He was there, Walt. He was wearing a white polo shirt, and he sat a foot away from you, and you were flirting with him, flashing your eyes, giggling."

"I'm sorry, I guess I just don't remember."

"I wonder if you were a different person," Steve said, touching his fingers to his desk. "Do you think so?"

"You mean like another personality?" I asked.

"Yes. Maybe."

"But I remember the lecture," I said. "I remember being there. I remember seeing you and giving you a smile."

Steve shook his head but did not take his eyes off me. "Walt," he said, "I think you ought to see a psychiatrist . . . you know, just to check on this."

"But you know my experience with psychiatrists," I said. "They don't know what they're doing."

"I've got someone in mind," he said. "He's the best. Really. Stanford. Harvard. He treated Joan Kennedy for her alcoholism."

"I can't afford a psychiatrist," I said.

"His name is Doctor Hawthorne. He'll work with you. I know that. Think about it."

Well, how can I possibly go to yet another psychiatrist? Don't you know I'm beyond Western healing?

I went home and studied the image of my favorite mystic, St. Teresa of Avila, her swooning figure penetrated by the divine arrows of love. I wondered if my pain was the same as hers, if my despair was exactly how I experienced ecstasy.

Still, I couldn't know. The torture continued. After a month I made an appointment with William Hawthorne. This time around, whether Hawthorne could help me or not, I was going to get to the bottom of things. So I drove to the University of Miami and bought a box full of psychiatric textbooks.

Then I met Hawthorne. He had the size and shape of my father and looked at me through his glasses with no particular expression. I looked back through fires.

"Why did you come to see me?" he asked.

"Mostly, it has to do with the fact that when I was little, Dad molested me," I said. I told him my story in a few sentences and then, when I got to my father's castration, he stopped me.

"Surgically castrated?" he asked.

"Yes," I said.

"And it was a family decision? No judge ordered it?"

"The courts weren't involved," I told him.

At our next session he told me that he'd researched the subject. "Nowhere in the medical literature could I find any cases like your father's. There just aren't any reports of doctors and family making a decision to castrate sex offenders. It's unheard of."

Why hasn't anyone told me this before? I had a flash. "I just now remembered something," I said. "I used to have impulses, to put my eyes out."

"When was that?" he asked.

"It was . . ." I thought for a moment, "right around the time Dad was caught and castrated."

"You know, Oedipus blinded himself," Hawthorne said.

My mouth dropped. Oedipus had torn his eyes out after discovering that he'd killed his father and married his mother. I knew in my gut that the blinding was a metaphor for castration. I'd done it to myself. Somewhere in my psyche, I'd taken responsibility for my father's life; I believed I could have stopped him a long time ago; I felt guilty, and I had psychologically castrated myself.

This was the first of a thousand discoveries.

At home I read my psychiatric texts and realized that I had a dissociative disorder. My mind—my consciousness—was split into parts. This protected me when I was a child: other parts of me experienced my father's touch, knew the despair, confusion, and pain. They developed ideas opposite mine. They hurt when I smiled. Some had no memories and no words, only poisonous emotions.

When a person dreams, he realizes that he dreamed only after he wakes. Sometimes, however, when a person dreams, he knows it and tries to wake himself up but can't. This is how dissociation interrupted my life. It interfered with my healing. I could learn something new, gain an insight, only to wake up a month later and lose my connection with everything I'd accomplished before. Sometimes I'd begin reading a new book, only to find it a month later under my bed, read halfway through and forgotten.

Everyone dissociates. It happens when people drive along a familiar or tedious route. They may daydream, only to "wake up" when they arrive at their destination, unable to remember the details of the trip. In a sense, their mind was operating in at least two states of consciousness: one mind driving and the other thinking.

I knew that the only way for me to heal was to know my states of consciousness. I needed to remember the journey that other parts of my mind had taken.

The melding began. One day at the gym I got on the StairMaster and suddenly froze in fear. I didn't know why. The same friends I saw every day were all around me, chatting and working out. But I stood there petrified, as if I'd been injected with a mind-altering drug. I looked down so that no one would see. I tried to control my facial muscles, but they fought against me. I waited until no one was around and left.

I saw Hawthorne and told him what had happened.

He asked me if anything unusual was going on that day.

"No."

"Was anything different? Did you see someone new?"

"No," I said. I began to replay the incident. "Wait . . . I just remembered: I was wearing a new pair of gym shorts. Like boxer shorts."

"Why would that make you dissociate?"

"I don't know." I thought about it. Then the memory blasted through. "On that camping trip when I was eleven, the one where Dad masturbated me, I awoke the next morning, stepped outside the tent in my underwear, and saw all these men looking at me. I panicked. I thought they were all going to get me."

Hawthorne nodded. "You were afraid of being raped at the gym."

"All because I wore a new pair of shorts."

Oddly, my mind was helping itself to heal. But therapy with Hawthorne became an unreachable thing, full of not knowing. For a full year I thought I was incurably crazy. I disintegrated everywhere, parts of me waking, sleeping, dreaming, dying. I feared that everyone on the island knew I was "off." I had no self-esteem, I knew it, and I tried to hide it. I talked to my friends, but a few seemed impatient, even angry with me for dwelling so much on the past.

This went on for years. I floated through layers of myself and into Hawthorne's office, never knowing whether the last session had been the real me or a dream state. He would not acknowledge different personalities in me and even refused to give me his diagnosis. I knew he wouldn't, because he knew I was suggestible, in the hypnotic sense. If he told me I had multiple personalities, I might seize on the idea, creating characters not only to please him but to ease my angst with the "fact" that my problem had finally been "identified." Physicians sometimes cause disorders (a process called iatrogenicity), and I am sure that Hawthorne knew he could have exacerbated my problem if he'd given me a diagnosis of any sort to cling to.

I knew, however, that if I were to integrate the parts of myself into me, I had to know what they were, where they came from, what triggered them. In essence, I believed I needed to see them as entities, with characteristics I could sort out and come to understand. They might as well be personalities.

But Hawthorne did nothing to encourage this. He said it was not necessary for me to name my states in order to heal. I didn't like it, but I knew he was right.

19

1993   I GOT A CALL FROM A FRIEND WHO'D SEEN BO'S PHOTOGRAPH in a fashion magazine. Seven years had passed since we last talked. I tracked his whereabouts to Miami's South Beach and called. He hardly seemed surprised to hear from me. He wanted to come visit.

When he arrived I saw that he was pale, beautifully tentative, more lovely and sensitive than ever. It was spring in Key West, the air sweet in jasmine, cool to the skin. We decided to walk to the community pool for a swim. No one was there. We lay down beside each other and looked at the sky. He asked me about Wallace.

"He converted to Catholicism," I said. "The embrace of the Virgin Mary, you know, she comforts him. I think he's happy—always challenging me with his higher wisdom."

Bo smiled. "And how's your mom?"

"She's doing okay," I said. "I think it was a relief for her when Dad died. He'd become such a burden toward the end. She kept her eye on him whenever children were around, even after he lived in a wheelchair. We're much closer now. She seems to have accepted everything."

For a moment I watched Bo. Why, after seven years, had he come to see me?

We lay still and unspeaking. We watched the clouds sail through. His skin was already pink.

"Why are you here?" I asked, unsure of my own question.

"I don't know," he said softly.

It didn't seem to matter. A thin cloud passed under the sun, shading the sky. Bo was peaceful; the hard cement beneath us seemed to push us up toward the clouds.

"Bo, how is your health?"

"I'm fine."

"You know what I mean."

He did not answer.

"It's okay, Bo. Please tell me."

"Well. Okay, Walt. I'm HIV positive." He sighed.

"Oh, Bo, I'm so sorry."

"I know," he whispered. He stared at me. He was too delicate to be sick. His eyes told me that he loved me, that he was sorry, that he wanted happiness. He was so light, I could almost see through his skin. I longed to hold him, but I also knew that somehow a greater thing would be realized if we just lay under the sky for a while. The memories came. A kind of grace, an inebriating peace wicked through our bodies. We were screaming, screaming through the universe, into the dark of space. I saw my panthers in the field. They had been waiting for me. I was amazed by their beauty. I watched them hesitate for a moment, watching me. Then they crossed over into a forest, as if they were being called.

Bo and I saw each other twice more, then he disappeared again. A few months later he called from California. He said he was in a wheelchair. He'd been diagnosed with spinal lymphoma. As part of a new treatment regimen, he was having the fillings removed from his teeth. Several months later his sister called me to tell me that he had died.

"How did he look?" I asked.

"He had the most beautiful expression, a release," she said. "He was so peaceful."

When she hung up, I cried.

I had things to figure out. I decided to go to Tallahassee and see what I could learn from Dr. Hahn. When I arrived, he invited me to his house, and we sat in lawn chairs in the backyard and talked about my father. Hahn was friendly, at ease. I wasn't.

"Dad told me a couple of times," I said, "that he thought his soul was caught in a tug-of-war between God and the Devil. I've wondered if you thought he had two personalities."

"No," Hahn replied. "But a lot of Tallahasseans, the card-carrying Christians, see you as the Devil. They say the Devil won."

"Because I'm gay?"

He nodded.

"Just before your father died," he said, "I was at a party, and I overheard a conversation. Someone was telling a small group that he'd been so perplexed and saddened by 'the most wonderful family that Tallahassee ever saw, a lovely wife and a father who cherished his community and gave of himself, and they had the most beautiful, sweet children you ever saw—and the son grew up to cast untold embarrassment on his family by becoming gay and leaving the family business and moving to Key West, driving his beloved father mad to bleeding ulcers and a heart attack.' "

Hahn leaned his head back against his chair. He was watching me. "That could have only been you that this man was talking about, right? They think the Devil won."

I didn't understand. I did understand, but I didn't want to. I felt pressure to leave.

Hahn was looking at me. "Right? It was you?"

I realized I hadn't answered him. I laughed, startling myself. "It couldn't be anyone else."

Several weeks later I felt an incredible urge to go to the Pacific island of Bora Bora. Nowhere else. I didn't know why. But I had to do it. Four weeks later I arrived.

The island floats in a brilliant green lagoon, puncturing the sky with one massive prehistoric tooth. The water around us was calm, but far out I could see a faint line, a surf rumbling in silence over the coral reef.

I'd found a hostel on the lagoon. My hut sat thirty feet from the water. I smelled the salt, the faint air of fish, the breath of the sun. The beauty was alarming.

On my second night I awoke with a pain in my throat. I couldn't swallow. I sat up in bed. Then, suddenly, a voice came. I couldn't tell whether the voice was my own or someone else's. There was a door. A boy stood in it, and he was looking into a room full of children. He told me their names. I looked at all of them and saw that they were me. The boy in the door told me about the time I was twelve and had to give an award to a philanthropist at a banquet. In full view of three hundred people I thoroughly wet my pants. He told me about other times I had forgotten. I was shaking.

I looked out of the opening of my hut to see if the world was real. The sun was a lie, tainting the lagoon. I had to go somewhere, somewhere. I picked up my bike and took the road that circles the island. Everything I saw and did provoked me. My lungs felt inside out. I pedaled around the island. By midmorning I found a hill leading to a cliff where huge boulders stood. I climbed up and looked down to the blazing green water. Something was wrong in the cross of light and stone, something awful. I stood at the edge of the cliff, sickened and drunk. I felt like I'd stood here before. Vapor swirled through the sky. I hurt too much to move. I sat down, keeping my head between my hands, resting, breathing. After a while I got up and returned to the hostel. I learned that I'd come upon a marae, a temple where ancient islanders performed human sacrifice. Had I read about this before? I didn't know.

I came back to Key West terrified of myself. When I told Hawthorne about the "midnight voice," I became nervous. But he seemed not to be interested. I felt too embarrassed to tell him about the temple. I wondered if I had made everything up, or half made it all up, or made up everything halfway.

Eventually, I decided it really didn't matter if the boys were real or not. What was important was what they represented.

All I knew to do was to keep reading and continue with Hawthorne. I told him about the weekend one summer during college, when my father decided to take two neighborhood boys on an overnight fishing trip. "He took along a fishing rod he'd given me for my birthday," I said. "And he dropped it overboard. When he came back from the trip and told me about it, I remember getting really angry."

"Why?"

"I guess I felt like the rod was part of me . . . a phallic symbol? Anyway, it was like he used me so he could get his hands on the boys. The fishing rod represented my youth. That was me he had out there, that was me he was using to get other boys. And he lost us both into the deep."

I suddenly thought of another boy, this one in my current life. I decided to tell Hawthorne about him.

"His name is Richard," I said. "He's about twenty, I think. He lives in a communal house with a bunch of hippies down on Whitehead Street. They're part of the rainbow tribe, very Birkenstock—you know, very cool. Anyway, it seems like Richard and I have some kind of connection between us, as if we can read each other's mind. Maybe it's that we're both runaways, maybe he was hurt in his childhood. It feels good to have a bond with him." Hawthorne seemed amused. I imagine he had a difficult time envisioning me, the conservatively mannered Walt, hanging out with a hippie boy.

We ended the session. As usual, I had ridden my bike to his office. I decided to take my time riding home. I stopped by a dock on the Atlantic. There was a breeze, and a million fine waves slipping past. Did they have something to say? Did they love me? I will never know, I thought. I smelled the salt air. I headed on, toward my apartment.

Halfway home, I saw Richard walking in my direction. I wondered where he was going. I waved, riding on, but he yelled at me.

"Walt! Walt!" he cried, signaling me to stop. "Wait! Guess what?"

I pulled over to the sidewalk. His eyes gleamed. He was so beautiful and full of amazement.

"Guess what I got in the mail today?"

"What?" I asked.

"A fishing rod!" the boy said. "My father sent it to me!"
I went home and cried.

There is no experience on earth like evening in the tropics. Islanders gather in scented gardens. Capes of stars sway over the sea.

On one such evening my friends had congregated on an open porch by the garden, nestling on a banquette like little puppies, drifting into the quiet midnight. I felt self-conscious. I sat by myself, upright against a wall, tense. That my friends could be so comfortable with one another made me envious. I'd never been able to let go like they could so naturally.

I moved over and settled between them. My friend Paul, on the right, slept on his side. I let my hand rest on his back. I relaxed the muscles in my arm and felt his warmth. Then I leaned against the shoulder of Dean. Now I closed my eyes and slowly let out my breath. I felt safe and at peace.

No one was making sexual overtures. No one was hurting me. My mind held together. I had awakened in a place where I belonged.

During our next session Hawthorne instantly recognized a difference in me. I suppose he could see it in my eyes. The trance—the appearance of a waking dream—was gone. It was as if I had been under water all my life, swimming toward the surface, never reaching it until now. Suddenly, I'd popped out into the world.

"I'm real to you now?" he asked.

"Yes," I said. "Amazing, how I hardly noticed you before today."

For the first time I felt compassion for Hawthorne. He was my friend.

Wearing a serene and tender expression, he asked me, "What are you going to do now?" I assumed he had decided that, well, I had healed.

"I'm not sure," I said. "For now all I want is to enjoy my life." I smiled.

The gift of being "here" took on new dimensions. Late in the fall of 1993 a friend and I took the boat out for the afternoon. We found some lobster and then, because we were tired, took a siesta on the deck. There was nothing else to do, nothing that required my attention. I closed my eyes and relaxed. Then I noticed the wind. At first it was nearly imperceptible, as if someone had gently brushed against my foot. It touched me again, now a luscious, living thing, whipping down my ankles, up my legs, caressing every cell and every hair. Now it rushed over my groin, crossed my chest, and then, like a child whispering a secret, it puffed into my ears. On impulse it turned away, on toward the sea. As if returning for more, it moved again and again over my body, each time leaving an extraordinary sensation of my human existence.

Until now I had only known about the wind. But today, perhaps for the first time since I was a small child, the touch of the wind was a thing I felt.

Still, I sank into depressions. At times I landed in my ice prison, never with warning, rarely with explanation. If I could just know why, maybe I could finally find some satisfaction, an acceptance, a release.

The poet John Malcolm Brinnin sometimes invited me to his condo for sunset cocktails. He knew that I desperately wanted to find meaning in my story. One afternoon we sat on his balcony and, with the churning waters of the Atlantic off in the distance, he asked, "Walter, do you remember the magic question?"

"No."

"It's found in the legend of the Fisher King."

"I don't . . ."

John Malcolm stopped me. He had a kind way of pretending to remind me about things I should have learned in college but didn't.

"He was a courteous and hospitable king," he said, "living in a magnificent castle with no apparent wife and with a peculiar affliction of interest to you: earlier in his life—while at war—he'd received a castrating wound."

John Malcolm took a moment to study me, as if to check on whether I was okay.

"His infertility is symbolically represented in the legend as a kingdom barren of life. You know T. S. Eliot's epic poem about this, *The Wasteland*."

I nodded. But I was actually thinking of J. Alfred Prufrock.

"Like your father, the king would distract himself from pain by going into his boat to fish."

"Really?"

John Malcolm smiled and continued. "One day Percival, who'd been wandering in the woods, came upon the castle. The king invited him in for dinner. Percival was quite dazzled by his surroundings. As Percival and the king were dining, a squire appeared with a lance, which oozed blood from its tip. Then a damsel followed, carrying a grail."

John Malcolm took a sip from his drink. I realized that I hadn't touched mine.

"Percival's curiosity was stirred, but in his youth he'd been cautioned that one can be too silent as well as too loquacious, and so he chose to keep his mouth shut. Well, Percival stayed on in the household. I suppose he was good company. One day a woman appeared at the castle. She was hideous—eyes small as a rat's, her nose like an ox—and she admonished Percival for not asking about the lance and the grail."

"Why?"

"Well, she told him that at the king's table the time and place was right for speech but that in an evil hour he'd kept his silence. Of course, Percival had no idea of what she meant by the evil hour."

"So what was it?"

"She told Percival that if he'd only asked about the lance and the grail, the king would have been cured of his wound and his land restored to fertility."

John Malcolm let the story end. I think he could see that I had enough to think about.

The lance and the Holy Grail are well-known symbols of the crucifixion of Christ and his redemption of sins. Percival didn't understand this. He had wanted to speak up, to ask a question. Who wouldn't, upon seeing a bleeding lance? But his awe of the king, his concern over propriety, fear of humiliation, his silence—these were inherent to the hour of evil. By not asking the magic question, Percival had allowed suffering to continue.

On the other hand, Percival really had no way of knowing that he should have asked his question. Therein lies the other lesson: evil has no reason. Evil is that the perpetual question of why has no answer.

One day I began to return to my old interests in science. Some new studies were suggesting that the prolonged stress of sexual abuse can cause such an abundance of certain hormones in the brain that they begin to— quite literally—excite neurons to death. They are called, appropriately, excitotoxins. If this were proved true, it would confirm my fears: no matter how much progress I made in therapy, it would never be more than a "work-around" of the damaged circuits in my brain.

I felt hopeless. I made myself leave the house to go for a swim down at the dock. The water was so green and glowing it looked like a sheet of light. I jumped into the water and began to swim. Great patches of turtle grass slipped beneath me. Millions of tiny fish clashed against the light, keeping me company, then fleeing. I swam about a quarter mile through the shallow water before I stopped to rest. I held my arms out to my side and floated on my back, looking into the blue sky. My sadness deepened. I hurt. I wanted to cry.

Suddenly, the lines of a Richard Wilbur poem, "Love Calls Us to the Things of This World," came to me: "And the heaviest nuns walk in a pure floating / of dark habits, / keeping their difficult balance."

At that moment I remembered how, as a child in a swimming pool, I had learned that if I held still, if I didn't panic, the water would support me. I didn't have to fight it, I didn't have to swim, I didn't have to do anything but simply believe I could float. The difficult balance was faith.

In 1994 I learned a bit more about brain science. Research seemed to be showing that even when neurons die, the remaining ones are able to make new connections with each other. Scientists called this quality "plasticity." It meant that there was hope, that neurons might find new paths through the scarred wilderness. I suspected this was happening to me.

I decided I wanted to see Hawthorne again. When I arrived, I sat down on the couch and stared at the books next to his chair. I held my head down, shyly.

"What's going on?" he asked me.

"I don't know," I said. "I feel strange. I don't think I'm dissociating now. I feel . . . kind of self-conscious. How strange."

"Are you embarrassed about something?" he asked in a voice most human and tender. He seemed to be talking to a boy.

"Yeah," I said, still unable to look at him, "that's how I feel, but I don't know why. I don't know what is going on."

"You're not looking at me," he said. "Do you know why?"

I looked up at him and then dropped my head, crying.

"Why are you crying?"

"It's just that . . . I don't know how to love you." I began to sob.

"Just let the tears come," he said. "It's okay."

I sat on the couch with my hands to my eyes, happy and embarrassed. Was this the first time in my life I had cried? Then I saw them, all at once, all the Walts, awakening. For an instant they sat in their classroom; they were real. I knew their lives. I understood everything. Then they vanished, and so did their world.

I don't know if at that moment my physical appearance changed, but I knew that something had happened inside me. I felt a tilt, a bloom, a sudden ease between one thing and the other—as a drawbridge drops over a tomb.

I awoke. I felt like I'd suddenly appeared.

Hawthorne watched me.

"This sounds strange," I said, "but I think I've grown up. I think it just happened."

"It probably did."

After this session we met a few more times, but our work was over.

20

I WANTED TO SEE MOTHER. SO IN THE EARLY FALL OF 1994, I WENT HOME to Tallahassee. I got in late on a Friday night and in the morning asked her if she wanted to go down to the beach.

We didn't talk much along the way. Since Dad's death I'd talked to her only on those days when I felt a little happy or encouraged. Now I wasn't sure if she was thinking about me, or Dad, or the roadside scenery. We arrived at the beach at midmorning. I parked the car under the shade of an old crab-apple tree. The cabin still sat on the dune as I remembered, squatting silently, as if contemplating a history of seasons.

Arriving here with Mother at my side felt both familiar and strange. I couldn't remember the last time she and I had come here. Whenever that was we had been strangers. I held so many secrets inside me that she had not even existed, not as my mother. But now we were here together. We got out of the car, she like a white gardenia, full of softness, no expectations but simple calm, just here with me, open and loving, placid, my blue-eyed mother. At seventy-one she still had a perfect complexion, hair the color of mist. She held no contrivances or affectations; she had aged honestly, a Southern lady who knew who she was.

We took our shoes off and walked slowly down the dune path to the beach. "My goodness," she said, looking around, "this is nice." She faced me for a moment, and I thought, she's looking for some sign of happiness. I wonder if it's there. I wonder if I'm happy or if something's still wrong with me.

I gave Mother a half smile and looked away. I felt uneasy, as if I needed to say something, but I didn't know what it should be. We walked toward the creek. When I was a little boy, a trip to the creek took forever. But we were already there at the bank, looking for a place to cross.

A hundred tiny sandpipers on the other side pecked the shore. We wet our feet in the cold water, tiptoeing through the creek. The birds suddenly ran, flying into the air. We watched them as they circled around back of us. We headed on toward the marsh, another mile to the west. Sand fleas jumped around our ankles, but they didn't bite. I didn't know what vein of thought to take. All I knew was here we are. Mother turned and looked into me, as if she was trying to recognize a mood, or notice a scar, or see how far my hairline had receded. I realized, well, she'd never really seen me before. I was her new baby, a son aged and young.

A dog came limping up. His hind leg was bent, hardly touching the ground. I saw a wound on his skin. He was old, a golden retriever alone on the beach. He came up to me and I reached down and patted him on the side. He ran up to the sea oats and grabbed a stick in his mouth and brought it back to me. I could hear his lungs; they had fluid in them and I thought he might have pneumonia. But he wanted to play, so I threw the stick. He fetched it and dashed back to me as best he could, tail wagging. I threw it twice again, and each time he came back, giving me the stick and rousing for another throw.

Mother looked at me. I looked at her. We grinned, because we both had the same thought, that we were being visited by someone from our past. The dog put his paws on my side. I laughed.

I didn't realize it until Mother and I talked later, but I had not smiled in her presence since I was a teenager. But now she saw it, the relief in a son she had so faithfully waited for.

The white sand stretched out to sea, the birds cried, the sky streamed around us. Suddenly, there were no shadows, just a ship in the distance. We watched it, slow and gray, until it was time to go.